Expert Systems
Commercial Exploitation of
Artificial Intelligence

IFS

EXPERT SYSTEMS

Commercial Exploitation of
Artificial Intelligence

Jack Hollingum

PA Consulting
Group

IFS Ltd, UK
Springer-Verlag
Berlin · Heidelberg · New York
London · Paris · Tokyo

British Library Cataloguing in Publication Data

Hollingum, Jack
    Expert Systems
    1. Business firms. Applications of expert systems
    I. Title
    658.05633
    ISBN 1-85423-042-5   IFS Ltd
    ISBN 3-540-53041-X Springer-Verlag Berlin Heidelberg New York Tokyo
    ISBN 0-387-53041-X Springer-Verlag New York Heidelberg Berlin Toko

© **1990 IFS Ltd,** Wolseley Road, Wolseley Business Park, Kempston,
Bedford MK42 7PW, UK and **Springer-Verlag** Berlin Heidelberg New York Tokyo

Phototypeset by Fotographics (Bedford) Ltd
Printed by Information Press, Oxford, UK

Preface

Writing a book on a subject developing as fast as expert systems is an exhilarating experience, leaving one somewhat breathless. Fortunately, the fundamental ideas are now well established, and the developments are in applications and in the ease with which new applications can be introduced.

This book has been written in the belief that it is important and urgent for senior managers in industry, commerce and government to understand the issues raised by the ability to store and manipulate knowledge, as distinct from data. For most organisations knowledge, which is for the most part stored in the memories of their key members, is their most vital asset, yet at the same time is highly vulnerable. Knowledge based systems, which are the subject of this book, give at least in part the ability to preserve and build upon the expertise which is so easily lost when somebody retires or leaves the organisation.

This is not a technical book. There are now plenty of books, as well as courses, conferences and software packages to help those who have taken the decision to become involved with expert systems. The purpose here is to explain in uncomplicated language what expert systems are; what they can and cannot do; how to get started and what it will cost – and to stimulate the imagination by describing some of the great variety of ways in which expert systems are now being brought into use.

The book is in two sections. The first section, written in close collaboration with the highly experienced knowledge based systems team PA Consulting Group, begins by spelling out the significance of expert systems for the future of business. It goes on to explain, for the non-specialist, the essential facts and terminology of experts systems, so that the reader will have some equipment for talking intelligently to specialists, vendors and software houses about possible implementations. It then offers some help in identifying suitable applications, and discusses different ways in which one can get started in using this new technology, and how the implementation can be monitored and costed. Section 1 concludes with a review of trends which could influence the development of experts systems during the next few years.

Section 2 of the book consists of a number of case studies of applications chosen for diversity in size, type of application and method of approach. Attention is focused as much on the reasons for going into expert systems and on the different approaches adopted as on the details of the individual systems. For the most part these case studies are based on personal visits to the companies concerned and discussions with the people directly involved with the implementations.

I should like to express my warm thanks to the many people in the companies named in the case studies who gave me so much of their time in explaining their experience – and their occasional mistakes – in learning about and successfully implementing knowledge based systems. In particular I should like to thank Royston Sargeant and his colleagues at PA Consulting Group who spent many hours in explaining the essential features of this new technology and its business and economic implications, as well as providing material for three of the case studies. We approached the project with the presupposition that if I could be made to understand what it was all about, then anybody could understand it. If the reader finds this book helpful, then the thanks must go in no small measure to the teaching skills of the PA team.

Acknowledgement

Section 1 of this book, and the expert system case studies of BP Chemicals' butadiene plant, the ISSUE intelligent spreadsheet environment and the PROTEUS club project, were written in close collaboration with Royston Sargeant and the expert systems team at PA Consulting Group.

Nottingham, June 1990

Jack Hollingum

Foreword

In less than a decade expert systems have grown from a position of relative obscurity to become increasingly important and practical business tools. Expert systems are a software technology which makes it possible for governmental, commercial and industrial organisations to process knowledge by means of computers. Its use extends the power and effectiveness of conventional data processing, and for some tasks it allows computerisation where previously this was impractical.

Managers are adopting this technology because they realise that successful organisations are those which can most effectively obtain, manipulate and preserve knowledge. Expert systems are the first popular, practical implementation of Artificial Intelligence. They are enabling more useful – and far more acceptable – computer systems to be adopted by managements in almost every sector of the business community.

Generally used in combination with traditional software, expert systems are providing both skilled and novice businessmen and women with support tools which really do seem to be intelligent. No threat is perceived, however, because unlike their human masters, expert systems have no intellect. Expert systems can't think – but they can know a lot, and help to make knowledge accessible to a wide audience.

So fundamental is the potential of expert systems technology that all managers should understand the benefits which these computer systems can bring to their own organisations. Those businesses which have already invested have done so for sound commercial reasons. The expert systems which they have developed are being shown to improve business performance and raise profitability. It is not surprising that little publicity is directed to the most successful projects by their owners.

Companies which have been first to use expert system technology expect to maintain a business lead over their competitors. This is because of the value and power of the knowledge bases which they have assembled – rather than the expert system software itself. Knowledge bases are business assets, have commercial value and are likely, in the long run, to influence company balance sheets.

There seems to be no limit to man's ingenuity in applying information technology to create business advantage. Expert systems represent a significant advance in pursuit of this ideal and are likely to change for ever the way in which knowledge is handled in our society.

Royston A E Sargeant

PA Consulting Group

Contents

SECTION 1

SECTION 1

1

EXPERT SYSTEMS – THE
NEXT BIG PROFIT-MAKER

HUNDREDS of millions of pounds are being spent in Britain each year on applying a technology which is still developing and has begun to prove itself in a number of small and medium sized applications. The heavy investment, though, is in anticipation of spectacular success in larger scale implementations which are under development.

The technology appears under a variety of names, of which 'expert systems' is the most popular – though, as we shall see, this is far from accurate.

Major companies – like BP, Shell, ICI, British Airways and Midland Bank – are heavily committed to its use and a number of smaller organisations are also becoming involved. The reason for the intense interest and massive investment is that these and other leading organisations have detected an opportunity for large gains in profitability for those who lead the way in applications.

Unlike many new technologies, where the wisest policy is to wait for others to do the pioneering and make the mistakes, those who are first with expert systems will gain a lead which will not be lost as further developments appear. This is because the essence of expert systems is that they provide a way of encapsulating 'knowledge' which, in the past, has only been available in the minds of a few experienced people – or in a less up-to-date and less convenient form, in books and manuals.

Knowledge may be simple and routine or complex and specialised but, once captured in a 'knowledge base', it becomes an extremely valuable asset which can be used in many ways and which will grow and be refined with the addition of further knowledge. Those who are first into expert systems will take the lead in developing large and valuable knowledge bases.

Expert systems have attracted some exaggerated and over-enthusiastic coverage in the popular press but there is not a large amount of factual evidence to support the enthusiasm. This is partly because serious applications of the technology – as distinct from demonstrator projects – are still fairly scarce but is also because the people who are successfully using expert systems are not really keen to share their successes with others.

The simplest way to give some idea of what expert systems are and what they can do is to give a brief outline of three practical examples which are described in detail later in the book:

● *Controlling a process plant.* BP Chemicals is currently installing a large expert system which is expected to raise the efficiency of butadiene production at its plant in Grangemouth, Scotland. The system will advise operators in the control room about the running of the plant. In particular it will provide early warnings of potential problems and give remedial advice in good time. As confidence in the reliability of the system grows, it may be allowed to carry out some of the control functions itself, simply advising operators of what it has done.

   The control room of the butadiene plant is representative of many large control rooms in chemical plants, oil drilling platforms and power stations. Fig. 1.1 shows such a control room at the ethylene plant at Grangemouth. There are, typically, several computer screens and a large number of indicators as well as lights and audible signals to give warnings of abnormal conditions. Some of these signals are of little importance or urgency while others are highly significant. The difficulty for control operators, with so much information being presented to them, is that they may find it difficult to make quick

Fig. 1.1 Control room at ethylene plant at Grangemouth (photo courtesy of BP Chemicals).

interpretations of what is happening and what the appropriate action should be. They can suffer from what is known as 'cognitive overload'.

A wrong or late decision does not usually threaten safety because there are automatic safety procedures which, if necessary, will shut down the plant. A shut-down, however, can be extremely costly in lost production. A large North Sea oil platform, for example, produces oil worth in the region of £1–3 million per day. A shut-down, even for half a day, is extremely expensive in lost production and in operating costs. Even an average process plant, such as an oil refinery, can lose half a million pounds from an unplanned shut-down for two weeks – and these are not as uncommon an occurrence as operators might wish. Added to these costly events are frequent minor losses of production efficiency which push up costs even more.

The expert system at Grangemouth, when installed in 1989, was believed to be the largest of its type in Europe. The real time expert system was designed to handle data from 7,000 process measurements and supervise up to 1,000 control loops. The installed cost of such computer systems is well over £1 million but it is expected that this can be recovered through operational savings in large plants within one year. The systems should help provide increased profits from then on.

- *Diagnostics on new products.* People at IBM's factory at Greenock in Scotland, one of only three centres manufacturing the PS/2 range of personal computers, have developed an expert system to help in the debugging of printed circuit cards and this is beginning to produce significant cost savings for the company.

  The problem for IBM has been that product design is developing so rapidly that circuit boards are liable to require redesigning or modification after as little as six months. As it can take test technicians up to six months to master the fault diagnosis of cards which have been rejected by the automatic test equipment, there was a very strong incentive to find a method which would help technicians establish the causes of faults.

  There are many diagnostic expert systems in use which capture the knowledge of experienced people and make it available to others but the difficulty at IBM was that, with a new product, nobody knew what diagnostic problems might arise, let alone what their solutions might be.

  The answer was to devise a system which allowed everything that was known about the possible causes of trouble to be made instantly accessible to technicians – design of the card, quality history of the particular card under test, details of similar diagnostic problems on other cards and how they had been solved, and so on. As technicians developed awareness of the most frequent causes of trouble and the most effective procedures for finding and dealing with faults, their experiences were incorporated in the growing expert system so that they could achieve a high level of competence more quickly.

  The system (see Fig. 1.2) was introduced in the spring of 1989 and IBM expects it to lead to a 20–30% saving in manpower as well as improved product quality, less fall-out from the line and enhanced skills for the test technicians.

- *High-speed service to customers.* John Crane International, the world's largest manufacturer of mechanical seals for pumps and compressors, makes thousands of different seals for equipment designed to deliver anything from milk to sulphuric acid or high-temperature gases. The company's technical sales engineers have to advise customers on the most suitable seal for each application and, until now, all they have had to help them have been their own

Fig. 1.2 Expert system on a workstation (right) assists technicians in fault diagnosis at IBM Greenock

experiences, seal selection manuals, fluid reference books and a bundle of technical data sheets – each continually being updated as users face the need to deliver new types of chemicals.

The idea of some sort of computer aid had been under discussion for some time but it was in 1984 that the company started work on an expert system to support the technical sales team in the selection of seals. It took until 1987 to develop a system which inspired sufficient confidence for it to be sent out for field trials in the company's branch offices. It was hailed as very interesting but, in fact, was not used.

This caused some fundamental rethinking about the design of the system and led to the creation of a system which can be used by engineers in whichever way suits them best. The system gives facilities for feedback of comments and their incorporation into regular updates of the system and it integrates the printing of a fully specified customer order at the end of the selection process. If a new set of technical requirements puts the selection task beyond the capability of the sales engineer, the system will automatically print out a fax message, giving all the relevant information, for transmission to the specialist engineer at company headquarters.

Delivery of the full operational system, to main John Crane offices world-wide, began in October 1989.

These examples are typical of many systems now being introduced into industry, commerce and the public services. They highlight several major benefits given by expert systems:

- Expert systems provide an efficient method for encapsulating and keeping knowledge so that it becomes an asset of the organisation.
- Knowledge can be made more widely available, helping to overcome shortages of expertise.
- Knowledge captured in an expert system is not lost when experts leave the organisation.
- Building knowledge into an expert system is something which can be done by people who are experts in their fields even if they are not computer specialists.
- Expert systems will do things which are difficult to achieve with conventional software. This means it is possible to automate many more tasks and provide facilities which were virtually impossible with earlier systems.
- The prototyping, development and maturation methods which have been devised for expert systems software will have a powerful influence on all computer software.

Developing and installing a large expert system is a high value operation – a system large enough to bring big returns to the user may well require an investment of tens or hundreds of thousands of pounds. The BP Chemicals application, costing more than £1 million, is a very large one from which very substantial benefits are expected. The experience gained from this project is expected to be applied in many other refineries, chemical plants and offshore production platforms during the next few years.

Until recently there was little scope for companies to arrive at a profitable implementation of an expert system – except through quite substantial investment. There were expert system 'shells' on the market, at quite low prices, but their capabilities were so limited that they gave users little more than a feel for the technology. Today, however, there is a growing number of tools available with a great range of capabilities, allowing companies to gain experience and confidence in the technology without huge initial outlay. It remains true, though, that any really worthwhile expert system will require a substantial commitment of time and effort.

WHAT IS AN EXPERT SYSTEM?

The name 'expert system' is inaccurate and misleading and it carries unfortunate overtones of 'mystery and magic'. It is used in this book only because it is in wide currency and most people think that they have some idea of what it means.

The systems considered in this book are much better described as 'knowledge-based systems'. This description covers a wider field and more powerful programming techniques than were found in the pioneer expert systems. It is also less emotive and more accurate. Knowledge-based systems do not use the same thought processes as human experts – they do not 'think' – nor do they really mimic human expertise. They simply store, in a sort of database, the knowledge which is put into them by humans – who may or may not be 'experts' – so that it can be manipulated, used to infer results and represented or applied in an orderly fashion as it is needed.

As it has become universally adopted, the name 'expert systems' will be used in this book but its meaning will be interchangeable with that of 'knowledge-based systems'.

Knowledge-based systems make use of techniques developed as a result of research in artificial intelligence (AI). This is a wider subject, largely still of mainly academic interest, but which includes, at its more practical end, such applications as image-understanding and speech-recognition.

One way of thinking about the simpler knowledge-based systems is as an extension of the trend in ordinary computer software. In a spreadsheet or database system, such as is used routinely by thousands of executives in industry and commerce, the information is separated from the computer program. So a single spreadsheet program can handle a great variety of financial, scientific and other data held in separate databases and manipulated by the program.

A knowledge-based system takes this a step further by separating not only data but 'knowledge' from the computer program, as shown in Fig. 1.3. In place of, or in addition to, a database the system has a 'knowledge base'. This can store not only numerical and simple alphabetical data but also more general knowledge about the task being addressed. The knowledge base can hold rules – e.g. 'if the car starter will not turn the engine **and** the headlamps are dim **then** the battery may be low' – and information about complete systems such as all the elements in a process plant and their relationships to each other. It can deal with concepts like 'too much' – for example, 'if the level in this vessel is too high **then** open this valve' – and it can cope

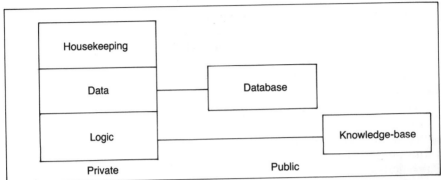

Fig. 1.3. The trend in computer software has been to separate first the data then the logic from the basic program, so that data and knowledge become accessible to the user

with the fact that a level which is 'too high' on one occasion may be 'too low' under different conditions, and so on.

So a knowledge-based or expert system has a software architecture in which both data and knowledge are separated from the computer program which manipulates them. The key part of the manipulating program is a piece of software known as an 'inference engine', the role of which is to work on the knowledge base, supplying logical ways of using the knowledge in the form of conclusions and recommendations. This separation makes the expert system structure much more convenient for handling complicated concepts. The structure is also highly adaptable because the knowledge base is in a form which can be accessed directly by people expert in the subject matter of the knowledge base – it is not concealed within computer code. The knowledge base can be continually expanded and updated to reflect more closely the situation in the real world.

Another highly important feature of expert systems is that they can explain the reasons behind solutions they produce. Some of the most impressive early successes were in medical diagnosis where it is important for a system to be able to list the logical steps by which it reached a diagnosis. A system at the National Hospital for Nervous Diseases, in London, used for analysing X-ray brain scans, is able to draw on a large and growing database of more than 1,000 brain scans for which diagnoses have been confirmed.

Several highly significant consequences follow from the ability of knowledge-based systems to explain the steps by which they reach a conclusion:

● A complex knowledge base can be built by a 'spiral' process of prototyping. A first attempt can be created and then tested by a number of experts who can detect any errors in the explanations given – even though they might have had difficulty explaining their own methods at the outset. With a conventional software system it would be unthinkable to produce seven or eight versions before the final one, because of the rewriting cost. For an expert system, seven or eight cycles in the development of a knowledge base would be quite a modest number.

- Knowledge is represented in an easily understood form. Conventional computer software can only be read by someone experienced in programming. A knowledge base can be presented in a form which allows it to be used and manipulated by anybody experienced in its subject-matter.

- Expert systems are always open to improvement and refinement. After the expert system is installed and running, an expert can study conclusions reached by the system and can make corrections or additions to the factual information or the rules on which conclusions are based. An expert system differs from ordinary computer software because it never needs to be frozen – it can always grow and develop in the light of further knowledge and experience.

- The systems can be adapted to altered circumstances. A knowledge base, devised to give advice on income tax liability, can be updated to accommodate changes in tax legislation whereas conventional software would have to be completely rewritten. Even before changes are incorporated it is possible, by tracing the reasoning, to detect where advice is incorrect and to make due adjustment. So, in a fluid situation, users can be warned quickly of specific points where the system may be giving wrong advice, before the knowledge base itself can be brought up to date. Meanwhile, the rest of the system can be working satisfactorily. Knowledge bases, therefore, are amenable to the concept of 'graceful degradation' of performance.

- Expert systems are valuable training aids. A system developed by one or more highly experienced specialists can be used by less experienced people and, at the same time, will help to develop their experiences and skills. Highly sophisticated training procedures can be incorporated, where there is no single 'correct' answer. For example, a diagnosis of a problem can be analysed, commented on, compared with alternatives and, if it is at fault, the consequences of the wrong diagnosis can be explained.

- Explanatory material can be integrated into the output of the system. A system, designed to advise on pension entitlements for instance, could write a letter to the enquirer, giving not only the answer to the query but also a complete explanation of the reasons for the answer. However, this facility needs to be treated with caution. There is a story, probably apocryphal, of a medical diagnostic system which was giving wrong advice and which, when queried, presented the list of reasons for its diagnosis. The user was so impressed that he accepted the diagnosis without further query.

WHERE MIGHT A KNOWLEDGE-BASED SYSTEM BE USEFUL?

The potential for applications of knowledge-based systems is very wide indeed and one might almost say, "The answer is yes – now what is the problem?" There are, currently, some economic limitations – particularly on smaller systems where the benefits may not be great enough to justify the development cost – and it is also unwise to give such wide scope to a system that its knowledge base becomes unwieldy.

These days there are two main reasons why people find profitable applications for knowledge-based systems, both of them connected with bottle-necks:

● The volume of work to be done may be greater than the number of experts available, either because of a simple shortage of experience or because it would be uneconomic to employ enough experts to deal with the peak of a widely fluctuating work load. Some expert systems have been developed because of the imminent retirement of somebody whose wealth of experience is unique or rarely available. Others have been prompted by a rapid expansion of business, beyond the capacity of existing experts and with insufficient time to train new people.
● If sheer pressure of demand on decision-making is too great it can produce cognitive overload. This type of problem is not necessarily solved by increasing the number of experts because they may need to consult with each other under conditions of stress, exacerbating the problem. The process control application quoted earlier is typical. Other situations which require complex decisions at speed include air traffic control and share dealing on a stock exchange.

In one case a problem is created by the extent of expertise needed while, in the other case, it is the concentration within a short period of time which creates difficulties.

Sometimes it is even possible for an expert system to enhance the knowledge of the experts who built it. This can happen where different experts have contributed to the creation of the knowledge base or where the expert system has access to a large and growing database to which different people contribute.

Other factors indicating scope for an expert system include: the need to obtain consistency of judgement between several people or over a large geographical area; the need to ensure that knowledge does not pass out of the organisation when people depart; and the need to train junior personnel without absorbing too much of the expert's valuable time.

Almost every branch of industry and commerce is, today, investing heavily in knowledge-based systems. In banking and insurance, people are finding many applications, for example in giving advice on share dealing, take-overs, mergers and tax, and in tailoring insurance proposals to the needs of clients. In industry, systems are being used to assist in design – of computers, process plant and other complex products – in equipment fault diagnosis and in scheduling and control of production operations. Medical diagnosis is a fruitful application area and there are many other situations where professional expertise can be captured in a knowledge-based system to a degree that at least allows the specialist to be freed from routine activities so as to concentrate on tasks which are more demanding of knowledge and experience.

CAN KNOWLEDGE-BASED SYSTEMS BE TRUSTED?

This is a sizeable topic, which is discussed more fully in later chapters, but a short answer would be, "They are as trustworthy as the information supplied to them by the experts". A knowledge-based system will normally operate in an advisory capacity – it will not take decisions on its own. One of its great merits is that it can be interrogated about its reasons for giving particular advice, and it will describe the knowledge upon which it has drawn and the process of reasoning by which it has reached its conclusion.

Human experts, looking at this chain of logic, may detect some incorrect or missing information which has led to a false conclusion and they can access the knowledge base to modify it so that the system arrives at the correct conclusion in future.

Much publicity is given to the dangers of fraud and malicious damage through devices such as the computer 'virus'. Expert systems are, if anything, less open to this type of misuse because their knowledge bases are open and accessible to all authorised users. False knowledge is, therefore, open to detection – it cannot be concealed in obscure computer code. Nevertheless, a company using expert system software is, ultimately, in the same situation as any other computer user – it must rely on the goodwill of trusted employees.

Another aspect of expert systems which raises questions about trustworthiness is the fact that a complex system may not be considered to be finalised when it is installed, in the way that conventional software would be fixed. A knowledge-based system can cope with situations which are far more complicated than would readily be handled by a conventional computer system. It can deal with judgements, uncertainties and probabilities. It can be continually refined and made to correspond more closely with the real world – the process known as maturation. In this respect, therefore, any expert system, except a very simple knowledge-based one, is never complete and perfect.

An ordinary computer program of equal complexity would require just as much work in debugging but it would be restricted to the tasks and assumptions for which it was designed. If there were any change in the real-world system which the program was modelling it would have to be scrapped and a new program written. A conventional computer program may, for example, work out a company's tax liability with accuracy and consistency but, if the tax laws are changed, the program will have to be largely rewritten. A knowledge-based system for income tax liability calculations would hold the details of the tax laws within its knowledge base to which an income tax expert would have access so that rules could be modified to accord with changed legislation.

SUMMARY

- Leading companies are spending millions of pounds on expert systems in expectation of substantial rewards.
- This is a technology where the first in the field will gain an advantage because it will have been the first to start building knowledge bases.
- News of applications is not widely available because successful developers are reticent for commercial or security reasons.
- Expert systems can do things which are much more difficult to achieve with conventional software and they provide an alternative approach to many software projects.

- Expert systems are a logical advance on database systems. A database separates the manipulating program from its data. An expert system also takes knowledge out of the program and stores it in a knowledge base in the form of relationships, **if** . . . **then** . . . rules and so on.
- The knowledge base of an expert system is open to analysis, refinement and growth with increasing experience. It need not become dated.
- A knowledge base is a valuable commercial asset. It makes the experience and knowledge of experts permanently and widely accessible.
- An expert system extends and standardises the ability to make sound decisions.
- Expert systems can provide on-the-job training for less experienced people, helping to overcome the problems associated with scarce human resources.
- An expert system can operate on complex data very much faster than a human, overcoming problems of 'cognitive overload' in difficult situations.
- Expert systems can be made as reliable and trustworthy as conventional computer software and better than most. They may never be 'complete', in the same sense as a conventional program, because their knowledge bases can mature – they are always open to refinement and updating. Like human experts, expert systems grow in usefulness as they gain more comprehensive knowledge.

2

BASIC FACTS ABOUT
EXPERT SYSTEMS

THE first thing that must be said about knowledge-based systems is that they are founded on well-established technology. They are not the latest piece of artificial intelligence to come out of universities and research establishments. In fact, research people have begun to lose interest in these systems because, to them, this is established technology and the emphasis has shifted to development and applications. For anybody thinking of spending money on a practical application this is good news.

The second important fact is that expert systems represent an addition to existing computer systems, an extra bundle of techniques, rather than something completely outside the experience of people involved with computers. The new techniques are powerful. New programming languages, new software environments and new development hardware have appeared to help in implementation and, for a company which already has programming expertise and needs to develop its own expert systems, there are short courses available to help competent computer personnel get started in this new direction.

It is not even essential to rely on people who specialise in computing. In some companies the opportunity for an expert system has been seen by a designer, an engineer or a marketing specialist who has taken the trouble to become acquainted with this very different branch of software engineering.

The third consideration is that expert systems require a new type of involvement on the part of user companies, whether they develop their own systems or employ outside consultants or software houses. This new involvement is associated with the commitment of specialist experts to the creation and maintenance of the all-important knowledge base.

ESSENTIALS OF AN EXPERT SYSTEM

An ordinary spreadsheet or database system, such as is used daily by thousands of managers with personal computers, can be described as consisting of a user interface, an application program and the data used in the particular program. The basic features of a knowledge-based system are similar but rather more complex. They are shown diagrammatically in Fig. 2.1.

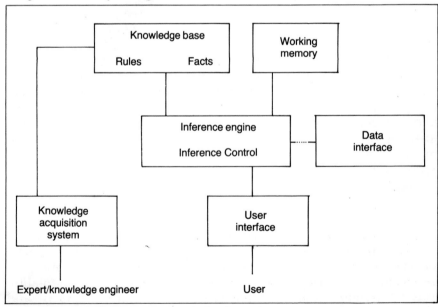

Fig. 2.1. Basic features of a knowledge-based system

(Knowledge base)

This is the most radically different feature. It (can be regarded as providing a model of that part of the real world which is addressed by the expert system. It may contain a description of all the elements in, for example, a process plant with their characteristics, functions, relationships with each other and so on set out in logical statements. It may also contain rules about the actions to be set in motion, as a result of certain events, or more conventional mathematical formulae.) It can point outside itself to external programs and databases which can be associated with it and some systems can cope with knowledge bases containing uncertain or conflicting judgements.

Part of the knowledge base, sometimes treated as a separate element, is the 'work space' or working memory. In dealing with a particular task or problem, the system constructs a number of hypotheses based on the external information supplied and on the knowledge and rules in the knowledge base. The current data, together with developing and alternative hypotheses, are held in the work space and updated as work progresses.

(Inference engine)

In smaller systems this is sometimes referred to as the 'shell' of the expert system, though the shell may be considered to be everything except the knowledge base itself. It is the software which uses the knowledge, represented in the knowledge base, in order to reach conclusions in particular cases. In simpler systems it may contain a defined strategy to be used in solving a problem but, in more advanced systems, the strategy itself may be contained in the knowledge base so that it can be refined and developed.) The design of the inference engine may limit the ways in which knowledge can be represented in the knowledge base so that certain shells are only suitable for particular types of applications.

(User interface)

This (is the aspect of the system presented to the end user) and it varies widely according to the type of application (The user may interrogate the system and the system, in turn, may ask for information or clarification to enable it to respond. The dialogue will generally proceed flexibly under the control of the user and the system may produce either a firm recommendation or some qualified suggestions.)

In any case the user should be able to interrogate the system about the reasons for its conclusions.

Data interfaces

This is one feature which expert systems share with database and other systems. Where the system is linked with, say, a process plant, most of the input to the system will come not from the end user but from the instrumentation and controls of the plant itself. Similarly a system giving advice on stock market trading would probably need to have on-line access to a database of market prices. Data interfaces enable this type of input.

Knowledge interface

A key element in a knowledge-based system is the software which provides a route for entering knowledge into the system and for checking, modifying and updating it. Traditionally this work was done by a specialist 'knowledge engineer', experienced in the creation of knowledge bases. He or she would interview experts in the subject of the knowledge base and reinterpret their answers in a form suitable for entry into the knowledge base.

With this arrangement it was not necessary to pay very much attention to the computer interface, as the knowledge engineer was well-versed in its idiosyncrasies. However, one of the features of successful modern expert systems is that, where possible, they give the expert direct access to the knowledge base at an early stage of the project. The knowledge engineer's role now, therefore, is to make this access as easy as possible – by careful structuring of the knowledge interface, in harmony with the expert's mode of thinking, and by providing a 'language' in which the expert can express knowledge.

The difference made by a well-designed knowledge interface is enormous. In fact it can determine the success or failure of an expert system project – if the expert can only build a knowledge base through an intermediary (a knowledge engineer), progress can be unacceptably slow and frustrating.

KNOWLEDGE ENGINEERS AND EXPERTS

In the creation and running of a knowledge-based system, four different roles can be distinguished and it is important to be clear about what these roles are and how they are described in this book.

Knowledge engineer

The knowledge engineer is a person who is experienced in artificial intelligence and expert systems and who may also have a background in mathematics, philosophy or cognitive psychology. He or she understands the various ways in which knowledge can be structured and should be able to create a framework for a knowledge base which is a convenient and efficient structure for the knowledge contained in it, reflecting the domain expert's way of thinking about the subject. In some cases the knowledge engineer acts as an intermediary between the domain expert and the knowledge base during the development stage but it is preferable if the knowledge engineer's skill can be directed towards helping the expert gain direct access to the knowledge base.

Domain expert

Domain expert is the name given to the person experienced in the subject matter of the expert system and whose knowledge is to be encapsulated in the system. This person may have no experience of expert systems or even of computers but he/she must have a good understanding and experience of the 'domain' covered by the system. Domain experts do not necessarily have advanced technological backgrounds or high intellectual understanding of the subject. In fact, 'expertise' may sometimes be a rather exalted word to describe their knowledge which may be partly intuitive. These experts must, however, be able and willing to collaborate with the knowledge engineer.

End user

The end user is often a different person from the domain expert – an operator in a process plant, a junior radiologist or a trainee in an insurance office. This is always the case where the purpose of an expert system is to make scarce knowledge available to more people. There are situations, though, where the system could be used by the expert, personally, to lighten the more routine aspects of a task or automating the simpler activities.

Sometimes there are different classes of end users, each with a different type of interface to the expert system. A system may be addressed by experienced staff, by trainees and by the general public. Each will want to use it in different ways and will need different levels of help from the system. The domain expert may also be a user of the system as well as requiring access to the knowledge base for updating.

Programmer

The term programmer is used here to describe the software engineer who develops the expert system itself, the shell for the knowledge base. The programmer may also be the knowledge engineer for a system but the functions are different. In any serious system, tailored for the user, there would need to be collaboration between knowledge engineer, programmer and user organisation but, with most proprietary expert system shells, the programming will have been completed in advance of the application.

HOW KNOWLEDGE IS STORED

The idea that knowledge can be documented, stored in a computer, manipulated and presented in a way that will help solve problems is attractive but not easy to grasp. We are accustomed to the handling of numerical data by computers, the simple manipulation of words in word processors and the routine arrangement of things like names and addresses in databases, but the concept of capturing knowledge, with its connotation of meaning, is more elusive.

Decision trees

One simple approach to storing knowledge, in use before computers came on the scene, is the decision tree which leads the user through a series of choices until a conclusion is reached. A decision tree can easily be incorporated in computer software and is one structure which can be employed in expert systems. However, its scope is limited because the user must answer the questions in the exact form and sequence in which they are presented. The system has no flexibility of interaction with the user.

Types of knowledge

To make real progress in the handling of knowledge, a distinction must be drawn between two types of knowledge:

- 'Knowing what'. This is knowledge of facts and relationships, for example: 'A bicycle is a type of vehicle with two wheels'; 'David is taller than Henry.' This is called *declarative knowledge*.
- 'Knowing how'. This tells what to do in order to reach a certain

conclusion, for example: 'To decide whether a vehicle is a bicycle, count the number of wheels.' This is called *procedural knowledge.*⟩

Another way of thinking about the distinction is to consider the differences between an ordinary driver's knowledge about driving a car and that of a driving instructor. The typical driver knows what to do when driving a car but may have difficulty in explaining this to somebody else. This ability is the particular skill of the driving instructor and it takes the form of declarative knowledge. The ordinary driver's knowledge is nearly all procedural. If there is a change in the highway code, the driving instructor can incorporate it immediately in his or her mental declarative knowledge base but the driver must learn new procedures.

Declarative knowledge takes the form of relatively simple and clear statements which can be added to and modified without difficulty. In order to use it there must also exist certain procedures – for searching through it, for deciding which knowledge is appropriate to particular situations and so on.

Ordinary computer programs, using languages like FORTRAN and PASCAL, take the form of procedural instructions and it would be possible to produce an expert system entirely on the basis of procedural knowledge, with the factual information embedded in the procedures. However, there are disadvantages in this method:

- In writing software, the same declarative knowledge may be used several times and in different ways. This causes not only the likelihood of unnecessary repetition but also the possibility of discrepancies entering between different uses of the same knowledge.
- If the factual knowledge in a completed system needs to be corrected or updated, it will be difficult to find all the references to it and the work will involve rewriting of computer code.

An early advance in expert systems was to separate declarative knowledge from procedural knowledge and to store the declarative information in a knowledge base, leaving procedural instructions in the inference engine. The more recent introduction of object-oriented programming has resulted in further changes which are discussed later in this chapter.

Rules

One way of expressing declarative knowledge is as a set of rules. For instance, 'if the person is employed **and** owns a house **and** has no bad debts **then** the credit rating is good'. A rule is, thus, a statement of a relationship, not an instruction. It is quite different from conditional statements like '**if** this is true then do that' used in procedural languages.

There are two ways in which an inference engine can attempt to apply a set of rules. These are known as '*forward chaining*' and '*backward chaining*' and they are frequently referred to in literature on expert system shells. In forward chaining, the inference engine starts from known facts and looks at the left-hand 'if' side of the rules, to find any that fit, and then goes on to look for further rules that follow on from those that have been found to apply. In backward chaining, the inference engine starts from the end – from the aim which is sought. So, it starts from the right-hand '**then**' side, to find any rules that satisfy the requirement, and works backwards to find what starting conditions are necessary to reach that goal.

Both methods have their advantages and are appropriate for different situations. In reaching a diagnosis from human symptoms or machine fault conditions, the forward reasoning process may be most appropriate. In other cases it may be more suitable to start from a hypothesis and to search for conditions that would produce that outcome.

Knowledge bases can be constructed entirely from a large number of rules and many expert system shells require knowledge to be presented in this form. It is an approach which lends itself particularly to diagnostic situations such as equipment trouble-shooting or medical diagnosis. There are, however, several weaknesses with systems which rely entirely or mainly on rules, which make them less appropriate in some situations:

- With complex systems the number of rules tends to multiply rapidly.
- As the knowledge base grows, inconsistent and conflicting rules may be introduced and, though there may be procedures for resolving such conflicts or presenting them to the user, the logical construction of the knowledge base becomes difficult to understand.
- There are many situations where rules are not the most convenient way of expressing knowledge.

Rules are usually one component of a knowledge base but they are generally restricted in number, as far as possible, and incorporated within a larger logical structure.

Knowledge structures

As the size of a knowledge base grows, it becomes more necessary to have some kind of logical structure within which the knowledge base can be built. One kind of relationship which often corresponds to a real-world situation is the tree structure. A process plant, for example, can be thought of as consisting of vessels, pipes, valves and so on. Each of these can be subdivided into types. Types, in turn, can be subdivided into individual items. Such hierarchies can be long or short, depending on the complexity of the system modelled.

Usually, though, a simple tree hierarchy is not adequate to describe the parts of a system. A valve can fit into a hierarchy of types for the purposes of describing its properties and performance but it also needs to be thought of in relation to its position and function in the pipework. Quite complex relationships are, therefore, needed between elements and groups of elements in a system. Specialists talk in terms of things like 'semantic networks', 'lattices' and 'association nets'.

Inheritance

One powerful concept which helps in the structuring of large amounts of knowledge, and the avoidance of duplication, is 'inheritance'. This is a technical programming term which relates to the need to create categories with classes and sub-classes, so that inferences can be made about individual items which are members of categories. For example, an expert system dealing with traffic flow could separate general knowledge about vehicles of all types from knowledge about individual classes of vehicles – cars, buses, lorries and so on – and, in turn, could distinguish between individual types of vehicles within each class. So, an enquiry about Ford Escorts, for instance, would call on the knowledge specific to Ford Escorts but it would also 'inherit' the knowledge relating to cars and to vehicles in general. Inheritance can be used to structure a hierarchy of rules but it becomes particularly important in more complex structures.

OBJECT-ORIENTED PROGRAMMING

A number of different words are used to describe the collection of rules, knowledge and data relating to a particular feature of the real world. Perhaps the most common expressions are 'frames' and 'objects', the latter expression coming into use with the introduction of object-oriented programming. (For non-programmers they can be taken to mean the same thing.)

A frame or object is a sort of receptacle for holding all the relevant knowledge on a particular subject together with information on its inheritance relationship with other frames. The frame may include factual information about properties, questions, rules and numerical data, and even procedures, hypotheses and mathematical formulae specific to that particular frame.

The frame also contains information linking it to other such frames, allowing inheritance of knowledge between them. The links may be of different types. For example, a particular valve may be thought of as one of a general class of valves, inheriting the properties of the class, but it also occupies a particular position in a process plant feed system and its operation will alter the flow of fluid.

Object-oriented programming describes a complete approach to computer programming, much wider than the subject of expert systems. The object-oriented approach, however, is a very convenient way of creating a knowledge base with concepts such as frames. It can also be used in writing the inference engine software but it is in the knowledge base that the effects are most marked as far as the user is concerned. Object-oriented programming can be used with standard artificial intelligence programming languages, such as Lisp and Prolog, but there are also languages, such as Smalltalk and C++, which are specifically designed as object-oriented programming languages.

Conventional programming separates data from the procedures which manipulate them. A conventional database program will incorporate procedures for reading, editing, listing and other functions and will operate by fetching data from the database.

Object-oriented programming divides up the task quite differently, creating 'objects' which contain both data (and knowledge when applied to expert systems) and the procedural code directly associated with that data. Each object is like a small self-contained program with its own database. Objects are simply programming devices. They do not necessarily correspond to any modelling of real-world situations but they offer a very suitable programming method for representing

frames. When the object-oriented approach is used in creating an expert system knowledge base, each object is like a small self-contained program complete with all associated knowledge.
The system works by sending messages between objects and an object responds to a message by invoking its own procedures. The object may, in turn, send messages to other objects in the knowledge base or in the inference engine, requesting information or action.

The flow of work in an expert system constructed in this way can be regarded as a series of conversations between objects. The inference engine, which can be constructed in an object-oriented style as well, provides the mechanism for inferring further knowledge from the knowledge already presented to it.

As an example, a traffic flow simulation will require representation of vehicles moving round the traffic network. Hence, a class of objects to represent vehicles by two-dimensional shapes might be created, with a position specifier, a method for changing the position and a way of asking for information about the position. This class of objects could be specialised into separate classes for different kinds of vehicles, such as cars, buses and lorries, with different graphical representations, different numbers of passengers, different priorities on the road network and so on. More separate objects could represent instances of particular makes and models of cars. To move the representation of a particular car round the screen, all this information would be called into use by an object representing movement with, say, a direction and a velocity.

One advantage of object-oriented programming is that it is highly modular and flexible. Objects can be created and tested separately as self-contained pieces of program code together with their own knowledge and data. They can also be combined and used in other objects in an economical manner. Where rules are needed, they are no longer lumped together in an amorphous mass but are incorporated within the objects to which they relate. This approach is most suitable for large systems because of its modular character and it is a natural programming method for frame-based expert systems.

EXPERT SYSTEM SOFTWARE

The computer program that operates on the knowledge base was described earlier as the inference engine. In a small expert system shell this is fixed and the knowledge base has to be constructed within set limitations. Larger systems have specially written inference engines and interface software which, though often containing many standard elements, are designed to work with the particular knowledge base structure and to carry out a large variety of tasks with the knowledge.

Today, most large-scale software development for expert systems is carried out on special machines which have the Lisp programming language built in and which can run special development software, such as Intellicorp's Knowledge Engineering Environment (KEE), and Inference Corporation's Automated Reasoning Tool (ART). KEE, for example, is a hybrid object-oriented programming system which can be used as a frame language but which can also incorporate a rule system, treating the rules as objects too.

Special development tools like these allow prototype systems to be developed very quickly. KEE is particularly useful for producing user interfaces quickly – a valuable characteristic when prototyping because end users often have difficulty in deciding which interface is the most useful until they can see and compare them. For example, Peter Clay, of PA Consulting Group, worked on a school timetabling system for which a prototype was required within 15 days. In that time he produced three prototype systems, in KEE on a Lisp machine, each, in turn, coming closer to a desirable system. The first was entirely rule-based, the second used multiple hypotheses and the third was mainly based on object-oriented programming.

After a system has been developed on a Lisp machine it is often desirable to transfer it to a more conventional type of computer. This is not an unduly difficult task although considerable effort may be involved. The conversion can be into conventional programming languages although there is a 'Common Lisp' language, containing all the fundamental features of Lisp, which is available on a number of mini and micro computers. Special Lisp development tools, like KEE, make available a 'superset' of Lisp, with many extra features allowing faster programming. If these features are used in development they have to be programmed out when transferring to other computers.

Another option is to build the expert system software from scratch, using a special purpose artificial intelligence language such as Lisp or Prolog. This approach requires specialist expertise in the particular language and is a laborious task, though there are now development tools available which assist in the creation of expert systems, using both Lisp and Prolog, at a lower cost than full-scale tool-kits.

Artificial intelligence languages are most commonly needed for research into new areas of application or where an expert system requires facilities outside the scope of commercial tool-kits.

The remaining option is to use a proprietary expert system shell. In the past these were severely limited, both in the ways in which they allowed knowledge to be represented and in the scope they allowed for tailoring the user interface. However, recent developments have widened the scope of some shells, bringing their capabilities – and cost – closer to those of the simpler tool-kits. There are shells available now which allow knowledge representation in frames and slots, with interfaces to a variety of programming languages, database management and spreadsheet systems and with quite powerful screen design facilities.

Distinctions in the hardware required for different types of software are also becoming blurred. This is partly because of the increasing power of personal computers (PCs). Major tool-kits, which in the past were only available for mainframe computers or workstations, now come in versions for 386-level PCs. On the other hand, shells, which were previously run on ordinary XT-level PCs, are now available in versions which take advantage of the increased power and capacity of new generation machines and there is at least one version for running on VAX computers.

BUILDING THE KNOWLEDGE BASE

Writing expert system software is a task for specialist programmers but, when it comes to building the knowledge base, a key role must be played by the person or people with experience in the particular field covered by the expert system – the domain experts.

In recent years there has been some debate about the 'knowledge engineering bottle-neck' being a problem facing the future implementation of expert systems. The reasoning follows from the fact that entry of knowledge into a knowledge base requires knowledge engineering expertise and knowledge engineers are scarce. In addition, the domain expert, who may know nothing about computers, must explain everything he or she knows about the pertinent subject to the knowledge engineer so that the knowledge engineer knows as much about the subject as the domain expert – inevitably a very time-consuming operation.

This method of building a knowledge base is also unsatisfactory in other ways. The expert's knowledge may relate to a subject which the knowledge engineer finds difficult to understand, so there is danger of misinterpretation. The inevitable delay, before the domain expert can test the knowledge that has been entered, also makes the whole process very slow and frustrating.

Some attempts have been made to turn the task into an automatic process – by supplying a computer program with examples of expert practice and allowing the computer to generate its own rules. This approach has been shown to work for small problems but its use rapidly becomes unwieldy as the complexity of the domain increases. (This technique is discussed further in Chapter 5.)

Another way of addressing the problem is to give the domain expert direct access to the knowledge base. This, however, places a new set of demands on the knowledge engineer who must anticipate the most appropriate structure for containing the knowledge and harmonising with the domain expert's way of thinking. The knowledge engineer must also create an interface which the domain expert can understand and experiment with.

This approach requires close collaboration between the knowledge engineer and the domain expert in the early stages of the project when the knowledge engineer is creating the framework for the knowledge base, entering sample knowledge and familiarising the domain expert with the method of working. After that, if the framework has been set up successfully, the domain expert should be able to enter and build the knowledge base, testing it frequently, with only occasional reference to the knowledge engineer.

A successful implementation of this approach, known as ISSUE, is described in more detail in the section of case studies. It was created as a result of a serious communication problem with one organisation which worked with PA on a knowledge-based system for share analyses. PA's knowledge engineers said of the domain expert, "We could understand every individual word he said but, when the words were put together, they didn't make any sense to us at all. We're pretty sure he felt the same about us."

Hence, PA created a screen display, which looked rather like a spreadsheet, with cells in columns and rows. Besides allowing entry of formulae and numerical data, as in a spreadsheet, each box could contain a logical statement or rule. Each row then represented a different company and each column represented either numerical information about the company or descriptive text covering character-istics such as management ability, share price relative to normal or future market prospects. A typical rule might then take the form 'if management ability is poor and share price is below normal and future market is poor then shares are not bought'.

An attractive feature of this method immediately became apparent. The expert was able to enter rules and immediately test their effects. If they gave unsatisfactory results the expert could modify a rule or add another rule to deal with discrepancies and recalculate all the cells to test the results again.

VALIDATION OF EXPERT SYSTEMS

Knowledge-based systems are just like any other computer software in that all standard procedures for checking the software must be carried out in full. The only difference with expert systems is that the knowledge base itself must also be checked and validated. This raises some interesting and important questions.

First, a large knowledge base is too large to test every possibility. It would be quite impracticable to attempt to reconstruct every possible situation encountered in a large expert system. Rule-based systems, in particular, are very difficult to check. A knowledge base constructed on an object-oriented basis can be checked more easily as it is created, but the larger it grows the more difficult it becomes to consider every eventuality. One technique which can be employed to cover the main possibilities is known as 'mutation testing'. Random changes are made to test data entered into the system to find out whether the errors thus generated are shown up by the expert system.

The second validation problem is that the system, unless small, is not intended to be finalised on delivery. A large expert system is not expected to be an immutable piece of software. It is designed to grow and develop as experience is gained in using it. On the other hand, the buyer of an expert system wants to be assured of a certain minimum level of performance by the time he takes delivery, though it is not easy to define even 'a minimum level of performance' precisely. The buyer also needs to be confident that the knowledge already stored in the knowledge base is accurate and consistent within itself, even if it is not complete. There are some techniques which can be applied to assist in validating a knowledge base – for instance, it can be tested for internal consistency and for completeness within its intended scope – but it cannot be said that this aspect of expert systems is completely clarified and further research to improve testing methods continues.

Finally, it is possible that some expert systems may contain matters of opinion. Some medical expert system knowledge bases, for example, may contain diagnostic information based on the personal experiences of one or more diagnosticians. In such a case, validation is partly a matter of satisfying the author of the opinions.

SUMMARY

- Expert systems are based on well-established technology.
- The systems consist of an additional range of software techniques.
- Elements of an expert system are:
  - The knowledge base, modelling the part of the real world addressed by the expert system;
  - The inference engine – software for accessing and using the knowledge base;
  - The work space, in which hypotheses are created and updated;
  - The user interface, through which the system can be interrogated and can offer advice and explanations;
  - Data interfaces – for example, to external databases, existing management information systems or to instruments and controls;
  - The knowledge interface, through which the knowledge base is modified, updated and enlarged.
- Knowledge bases are created through collaboration between the *knowledge engineer*, a specialist in knowledge structures and software, and the *domain expert* experienced in the subject matter of the expert system.
- Knowledge may be stored in various structures, including *rules, frames* and *slots*, analogous to database records and fields, and association nets.
- Object-oriented programming is an approach to programming which is particularly convenient for creating knowledge bases.
- Special hardware and software tools are available which assist the speedy prototyping and development of expert system software.
- There are powerful advantages in creating a knowledge interface which will allow the domain expert direct access to the knowledge base.
- Validation of expert system software requires the same procedures as for any other software.
- Validation of the knowledge base raises new issues:
  - A large knowledge base has far too many options for every one to be tested;
  - A knowledge base is essentially incomplete when first installed and is continually enlarged and modified in the light of experience.

3 EXPERT SYSTEMS AND YOUR BUSINESS

ANY company that is using computers and relies to any extent on its own knowledge should, today, be seriously investigating expert systems because they have the potential to be of strategic importance to business.

ENHANCE COMPETITIVE STRENGTH

One of the first highly successful expert systems was that introduced in 1980 by Digital Equipment Corporation for configuring its VAX computers. The task of dealing with a customer's order, which might consist of 30-40 different major items built from more than 5,000 components in many different ways, had become extremely difficult because of modifications necessary to combine the items satisfactorily. There were delays in handling orders and many mistakes in the internal ordering of such things as cable lengths.

With its XCON expert system, DEC was able to reduce 20-30

minutes of a highly skilled configurer's time to less than three minutes of computing time, and the system prints out a very detailed ordering list, with details of any modifications needed to the customer's original specification. The system also prints layout diagrams, showing the placing of components within cabinets and exact cable lengths required.

According to DEC, the savings from introducing XCON were far more than simply the reduced time in handling customers' orders. Previously, many incomplete computer systems had been scheduled to the factory, often with configuration errors, resulting in serious production losses. With XCON, 98% of factory orders are very accurate. The result is faster throughput, better material utilisation and better delivery. That, though, is only the beginning. Senior technicians are now free to concentrate on important technical tasks and the company is better able to respond to growing and changing market demand.

The company's conviction about the competitive value of expert systems is reflected in the fact that XCON has been continuously extended and updated. By 1988, the original system, with 700 rules dealing with 400 components in a single type of computer, had grown into a system with more than 10,000 rules handling a database of more than 30,000 components belonging to 30 computer system families.

SAFEGUARD AND DEVELOP KNOWLEDGE

There is a temptation for manufacturing companies to assume that most of their knowledge resides in drawings, process planning sheets and similar paperwork. In fact, these simply allow the continuation of what was done in the past and, in any case, cover only a part of a manufacturing company's operation. Most of the knowledge required to run any organisation is in the skills and memories of people in that organisation. This fact becomes all too apparent when a key person leaves or retires.

Knowledge-based systems give, for the first time, the ability to capture and store some of this knowledge in a way that allows it to be recovered and reused in new circumstances. Thus, it is not entirely lost with the departure of the person who originally acquired the knowledge. More than this, expert systems can bring together the experiences of different people and can even highlight and help resolve differences of interpretation. As time passes, the knowledge base continues to grow, accumulating more knowledge than one person can easily recall. Many specialists in artificial intelligence are currently saying that as expert systems acquire very large knowledge bases they will begin to exhibit the characteristics of 'intelligence'.

An important feature of a diagnostic system for printed circuit cards, developed by IBM at Greenock and described more fully in Chapter 6, is that it not only makes accessible a great volume of information held in drawings and reports but it also gives test technicians access to 'soft' knowledge which had previously been carried in the heads of designers and test engineers, not written down.

KNOWLEDGE AS A CAPITAL ASSET

As knowledge bases grow they become an increasingly valuable property of the company or organisation holding them and they can be expected to appear soon in company balance sheets as assets. They also become a saleable commodity. One can envisage, for example, a wide market for an income tax adviser system or a knowledge base to help in designing central heating systems.

One expert system, giving advice on design for assembly, developed by Lucas Engineering & Systems in collaboration with Dr. Ken Swift of Hull University, was originally intended for use within the Lucas Group but it has now been placed on the open market and is supported by teaching seminars. (This system is described in the case studies in the second section of this book.)

KEEPING KNOW-HOW UNDER WRAPS

It can be made difficult for unauthorised people to acquire the knowledge held within a knowledge base and this is important to organisations which want to lease the right of access to a knowledge base without giving up control of it.

A processing company, for example, may reach an agreement to set up a plant in a Third World country. Nowadays, as part of the agreement, engineers from that country would be trained in the running of the plant and, in doing so, would gain expertise which had been acquired over many years by the processing company. If the expertise in running the plant is embedded in an expert system, the relevant parts of the system can be provided as part of the agreement and this will give the user the benefit of all the supplier's expertise. This could also involve regular updating of the system as part of the agreement.

However, the knowledge itself would remain in the knowledge base and would be virtually impossible to reconstruct for the same reasons that it is impossible to validate a knowledge base completely – there are too many possible situations that can arise and too many questions that would have to be asked of the system to extract more than a small proportion of its knowledge.

With this sort of access agreement, both parties stand to gain – the customer from having a reliable and efficient plant, without the need to develop and rely on scarce operating expertise, and the supplier in keeping control of the knowledge on which the efficient running of new plants depends.

OPTIMISE EXPENSIVE AND DANGEROUS PROCESSES

Where an operation or process needs extremely close and continuous control, either because departures from optimum are very costly or because it is potentially hazardous, a knowledge-based system supporting those running the plant can bring very substantial benefits. The LINKman system, developed by Blue Circle Industries and Sira, has been installed at a number of cement kilns operated by Blue Circle. At Blue Circle's Hope works, where it was first installed, the system is achieving savings of an 80 tonne/hour process cement through better process control of an 80 tonne/hour process cement kiln. To optimise the kiln operating conditions the system mimics the methods used by operators but its speed of reaction to data coming from the kiln instrumentation allows it to run the plant stably at a lower temperature than can be maintained by the operators.

IDENTIFYING APPLICATIONS

Almost any computer system would be more effective as a knowledge-based system, if only because the maintenance and updating of the system is transferred from the computer specialist to the domain expert. The task here is really one of identifying those applications which will justify the expense of setting up a knowledge-based system. The correct approach, therefore, is not to search for applications which will provide an excuse for trying out this new technology but to add knowledge-based systems technology to the armoury of computer aids that can be brought to bear on the company's problems.

As pointed out in the first chapter of this book, most expert systems find applications where there is a bottle-neck of experience – either because of the complexity of decisions that must be taken within a limited time or because there are not enough experienced people for the scale of the task.

Lack of time

Time is a constraint in the control of complex plants like nuclear power stations or in air traffic control. It can also impose restrictions in the handling of goods. For example, in sending perishable goods by sea, an event, such as a dock strike, could prevent a ship unloading at its intended destination. A decision would have to be taken to send the ship to some other port which could be reached within the time limit and at which a satisfactory price could be obtained for the goods.

Similarly, in a large school, updating the timetable at short notice, to allow for staff illnesses, is a difficult task which cannot be overcome by sharing the job among more people. Problems like these arise throughout industry and commerce when staff must be reallocated to maintain priorities with minimum disruption of other tasks. Scheduling of drivers and lorries in a large distribution network, for instance, is made more difficult and potentially less efficient by changes at short notice – staff and vehicles becoming unavailable, last minute changes in customers' orders, route changes because of traffic conditions and so on.

Shortage of experience

Most opportunities for knowledge-based system applications arise from the other type of bottle-neck – where there are not enough experienced people and, for some reason, they cannot be hired or trained. Here, a system may be used by the expert to take over routine tasks, leaving him or her free for the more difficult decision-making. It may also allow less-experienced people to carry out tasks usually requiring greater expertise while, at the same time, developing their skills. The opportunities here are very wide indeed.

Limiting boundaries

The first thing to check when considering a possible application is that the task has clear-cut boundaries which are not too wide. The knowledge base will have to contain a workable model of that part of the 'world' which is being simulated in the expert system. Also, if it is difficult to decide what concepts could influence the working of the system – particularly if the number of relevant concepts is large – the knowledge base might need to be impossibly huge.

Many simple decisions

One situation where application of a knowledge-based system may be worth investigating is where there has to be repetitive decision-taking at a fairly low level. One example could be insurance underwriting. Of, say, 100 requests daily, 80 may be obviously acceptable and 10 obviously unacceptable, leaving only 10 requests where the under-writer must investigate more deeply and use specialist expertise. An expert system could be developed to handle the 90% of cases which are clearly acceptable or unacceptable and to write an individual letter to each applicant, leaving the underwriter free to deal with the difficult cases.

Conversely, a problem which recurs only occasionally, however amenable in principle to knowledge-based system treatment, is unlikely to prove economically viable for application unless other customers can be found for it. One can envisage a system for assisting a company in long-range strategic planning but it would probably not be used often enough to justify the cost, unless it could be distributed among a number of member companies in a group.

Frequent changes in knowledge

Another sign of what could be a worthwhile application is if the knowledge is changing fairly frequently. Conventional computer systems have knowledge built into the program and any change in the knowledge they must employ, as distinct from the data they must use, will require a modification of the software. Examples are diagnostic systems, where the design of the product being diagnosed is subject to change; sales and distribution systems, for the same reason; and production scheduling, where equipment availability and sub-contract facilities are changing frequently.

Multiple use

The economic case for an expert system can sometimes be strengthened if there are a number of different applications to which a single knowledge base can be put. A system to give advice on pension rights could, for instance, have different user interfaces for access by pensions advisers, by trainees and by the general public, each group having different levels of experience and wanting to interrogate the system in different ways.

Digital Equipment's XCON system, for use by computer configuration specialists, has been supplemented by another expert system, XSEL, which makes use of the same knowledge base and component databases but is a smaller system designed to support the company's sales people. XSEL helps them advise customers on the most suitable computer configurations and it prepares accurate price quotations. Digital estimates that XSEL and XCON, together, have saved the company $40 million in direct costs and have increased order accuracy from below 70% to 98%.

Formulation difficulties

Sometimes a situation arises which would benefit greatly from computer assistance but where difficulty is experienced in formulating the task for coding into a conventional computer program. The flexibility offered by a knowledge-based system and the opportunity for discussion and explanations between the domain expert and a knowledge engineer may help to clarify the task. The prototyping opportunities offered by expert system software also allow the user to approach the problem in different ways while trying to reach a workable model. The Digital XCON configuration system quoted earlier was just such a case, where there had been a number of attempts to computerise the task by conventional means before the expert system approach was adopted.

Typical of cases where a conventional solution is virtually impossible are situations where the domain expert uses vague rules of thumb, where a decision depends on weighing up the likelihood of different things happening, any situation where knowledge is incomplete or where there are many acceptable outcomes but some are more desirable than others.

Explanation required

The ability of an expert system to explain its conclusions in detail may be a decisive factor in adopting this approach, particularly in training situations or where the system is drawing on a very large database of abstruse information which no individual person could hold in memory. Medical diagnosis is one obvious example and this is also a case where factors outside the scope of the expert system can enter into the final decision.

Consistency

In complex decision-making one expert may come to different conclusions at different times on the same matter. Given the same initial conditions, an expert system will always reach the same conclusion, giving consistent advice on matters of judgement. An expert may decide that the system has reached a wrong conclusion, in which case the knowledge base can be modified to give, consistently, a different conclusion.

ESTIMATING THE COST

In most cases it is economics rather than technical considerations that will stand in the way of expert system applications. The only serious technical limitation mentioned above – and even that could be described as economic – is that as the scope of a knowledge-based system increases, in the direction of 'life, the universe and everything', it has to acquire a memory approaching that of the human brain and, probably, a processing speed well beyond the scope of present technology. A large knowledge base is necessary for the more interesting applications but there are limits to what is achievable.

Expert systems are generally, though not always, high-value technology. Hardware and software costs for major tool-kits add up to tens of thousands of pounds. Simple expert system shells, suitable for gaining a basic understanding of the technology, can be obtained for a few hundred pounds but shells suitable for creating small practical systems generally cost more than £1,000.

However, the major expense for a company investigating expert systems will be in people and this is true whether the company decides to develop its own expertise or go to an outside organisation for help. The greater part of this manpower cost may well be in the valuable time of experts who are needed to build the knowledge base rather than in the software cost of an inference engine or shell. To reach the stage of having a useful system producing worthwhile results it is likely that an overall investment of £100,000 or more – sometimes much more – will be needed.

A small investment in expert systems is unlikely to produce results sufficient to justify it and some of the lower-cost shells have such restrictive knowledge representation facilities and poor interfaces that they may even discourage the user from attempting anything more ambitious.

As the cost of entry is relatively high, the prospect for small expert systems, to deal with such matters as professional assistance, is not very good – unless a company can see an opportunity for marketing such a system widely, at a price commensurate with its utility, or a trade or professional association makes the investment in a system on behalf of its members. In some cases it may be possible to create a purpose-designed shell, with a small knowledge base of common knowledge, which could be grown by members of the organisation into worthwhile systems, tailored to individual requirements.

Some examples are given, in Chapter 6, of 'club projects' in which the cost is shared by a number of organisations with similar interests. As long as the 'club' has a clearly defined expert system as its objective, rather than a general familiarisation with the subject, such a method can be a relatively inexpensive way of obtaining something close to requirements.

GETTING STARTED

For any organisation which thinks it may benefit from expert systems, the first step will nearly always be to appoint a senior person to acquire a general understanding of what expert systems are and what they can do. There is no particular need for the person to be a computer specialist. The natural choice would be a person from the department which stands to gain most from the introduction of expert systems. It could be the data processing department but it could equally well be a sales department, research and development, engineering, manufacturing, quality or maintenance.

The person appointed should be one who can be a powerful champion of the cause if it is seen to be worthwhile. Somebody who has access to top management, is prepared to face criticism and is well able to present and argue the case. This is particularly important because it is often found that the initial response from middle management is strongly negative.

The person appointed will probably start by going on one of the many short courses on expert systems, doing some background reading and, possibly, attending one of the increasing number of conferences on the subject. It is also very useful to find and visit other companies, in the same or related industries, which are already using expert systems.

As previously stated, it is not necessary for the person investigating expert systems to be a computer specialist, although it is advisable to have somebody who is computer literate to the extent of being acquainted with the broad terminology. Far more important is a good understanding of any practical problems within the organisation which might benefit from expert systems. There is certainly no need for in-depth study of special-purpose artificial intelligence languages or tool-kits unless the company is going to develop its own expert system software.

From this point there are several possible ways to proceed. It may be that there is a trade or professional association which is studying expert systems on behalf of its members. It may even be running a collaborative development project from which the company would gain at least more knowledge if not the basis for a working system.

In the recent past, another way for companies to gain some understanding and experience of the potential for expert systems within their organisations has been through Alvey clubs. These were set up under the government-supported Alvey programme for promoting collaboration between industry and the academic world in the development of information technology. In 1990 the clubs are coming to the end of the their programmes but several 'post-Alvey' clubs have been created to continue collaborative work on experts systems, in particular fields of activity. These new clubs are, generally, more precisely focused on the development of a practical system than were their predecessors.

In the case studies at the end of this book there is a description of the PROTEUS Club which has been sponsored by the Department of Trade and Industry and which is supported by organisations interested in the development of an expert system to assist in the purchase of very large computer systems. The amount of benefit a company gains from membership of such a club depends entirely on the amount of effort it puts into it. Simply receiving and reading the report papers will do little to advance the company's involvement but active participation should, at least, help a company to discover the main players in the game and their usefulness to the company's interests.

Another way to get started, without too great a financial commitment, is by acquiring one or more commercial expert system shells. These are relatively inexpensive and most of them are not too difficult to understand and use. It is important to bear in mind, though, that the initial cost of the shell will be small in comparison with the cost of building the knowledge base and that it is essential that the particular shell chosen should be capable of creating the type of expert system the company needs.

Most expert system shells were originally developed from individual applications using rule-based programming. Examples of such systems include: DENDRAL, for analysing chemical structures; MYCIN, for giving advice on the selection of appropriate antibiotics for blood infections and meningitis; and PROSPECTOR, for giving expert advice in mineral exploration and resource evaluation. Such shells are well suited to dealing with classification problems like medical diagnosis, tracing faults in equipment and other problem-solving tasks of this kind.

If a shell can be found which fits the domain to be covered by an expert system it, at least, allows a prototype system to be developed very quickly and effectively, so can be a persuasive ambassador for the cause of expert systems in an organisation. For a relatively small system, the shell itself may be adequate. If, on the other hand, the ultimate system is beyond the scope of a chosen shell, at least the company will have gained a better understanding of what it wants to achieve with a system.

Some rule-based shells have recently extended their capabilities by addition of rule induction facilities. With such a facility, a number of sample situations and solutions are presented to the expert system which then induces a set of rules to satisfy the sample problems. This method can be useful where a user has a large amount of case material but would have difficulty in defining rules to cover the cases. However, the rules tend to increase rapidly in number and complexity as more samples are added and a system using this procedure is not very good at explaining its conclusions because the rules it has induced are not based on natural human thought processes.

Induction systems also tend to be inefficient at generating knowledge which uses intermediate concepts. For example, a process plant system may require the concept of viscosity which may be derived from information embedded in rules about the material, its temperature and so on. This intermediate concept can then be used in further rules, related, say, to the performance of a pump. A system built by induction from examples would by-pass the intermediate concept and would refer pump performance straight back to the fundamental factors. It might mimic the expert's performance satisfactorily but it would not be able to give clear explanations in terms of the intermediate concepts.

A few shells, which have become available on the market recently, make use of an object-oriented approach, giving them a wider scope for applications even though they require rather more technical skill and training than rule-based systems. In effect, they are beginning to bridge the gap between shells and the artificial intelligence tool-kits described in the previous chapter. A good shell will offer one or two 'paradigms', such as rules and semantic networks, for constructing knowledge bases and some limited facilities for developing the man-machine interface and interfaces to other equipment and software. A tool-kit will support a number of interface paradigms and knowledge base paradigms but it will probably need to be run on a special-purpose workstation – and it will be very expensive.

Large companies which see substantial benefits from knowledge-based systems can afford to train and keep their own teams of specialists in artificial intelligence technology. They will probably need to equip the teams with dedicated workstations and artificial intelligence tool-kits but this sort of expense can only be justified if there is a steady flow of work.

Most companies and organisations will probably find it best to get started by acquiring some general knowledge and by following this up with experimenting with a shell or joining an expert system club. When the company has identified an area which is likely to provide a worthwhile application, it will probably approach a consultancy or software house specialising in expert systems, with a view to developing a prototype system.

Developing a prototype is not costly and it will give a clear indication of what a full system can be capable of, as well as allowing a realistic cost benefit exercise to be carried out. The steps in prototyping and implementing a system are discussed in the next chapter.

Sometimes, even very large companies adopt this approach, putting their own engineers alongside a consultancy's specialists, so that the engineers acquire experience in building an expert system while, at the same time, a system is developed for them.

SUMMARY

- Expert systems have strategic consequences for your business:
  - They can enhance its competitive strength;
  - They allow knowledge to be safeguarded and developed;
  - Knowledge becomes a capital asset;
  - The use of knowledge can be sold while retaining the knowledge itself:
  - Expensive and dangerous processes can be optimised.
- Applications are mostly where there is a bottle-neck of experience, either because of time constraints or through a shortage of experts.
- Limitations on practical applications are mostly economic – seldom technical.

- Profitable applications are usually of a size that requires an overall investment in excess of £100,000.
- The first step towards introducing expert systems will probably be to appoint a senior person who will investigate the opportunities and will champion the cause if there are likely applications.
- Initial experience may be gained by membership of an expert system club or by experimenting with an expert system shell.
- For most companies, implementing a practical system will require the help of a specialist software house or consultancy.

4 IMPLEMENTING AN EXPERT SYSTEM

ASSUMING that somebody who carries weight in an organisation has an understanding of what can be achieved with expert systems and has identified one or more situations where a system might prove beneficial, the next step will be to test the tentative conclusion by developing a prototype application.

PROTOTYPING

If a shell, congenial to the type of application envisaged, has been found this can provide a low-cost way of proving the feasibility of a full-scale expert system. The difficulty with this approach is that one may not know in advance what types of knowledge base and interfaces need to be created, and a shell can offer only a limited range of choices.

Probably, the method most likely to lead to a successful outcome is to collaborate with a software house or consultancy specialising in the development of expert systems. Such an organisation will very likely have access to one of the powerful but expensive artificial intelligence (AI) tool-kits which allow prototyping to be done quickly, efficiently and with very high flexibility. The organisation may also have experience with a number of different shells and be able to select one suitable for the particular application being considered.

Choosing a firm of specialists to carry out a pilot project is much the same as in any other activity. It is wise to look for a company that has done something similar before and to go and talk to the relevant client. If that leads to a favourable impression of the specialist organisation then it is reasonable to ask for the same software engineer or team who did the work for the previous client, and to talk with them to find out whether they are the kind of people your organisation can work with.

The main purpose in prototyping is to ensure that the project is feasible and to gain some idea of the ultimate cost and the benefits that can be expected from it. The prototype should give a feel for the way the ultimate system will work, by offering a reasonably realistic user interface. If, at this point, it is decided not to proceed, the cost should not have been more than between £5,000 and £25,000, depending on the size of the project, and a useful insight will have been gained into the way knowledge-based systems work.

Building a prototype may take two to three weeks using a powerful development environment, such as a Lisp machine with KEE, or with the help of a suitable shell. The resultant system will provide an outline model of the domain covered by the proposed system and will incorporate sample interfaces and a rudimentary knowledge base. A prototype will probably use some programming short-cuts to present something that will work, albeit in a limited way, like the real thing, to give an appreciation of what can and cannot be done.

Prototyping will reveal what problems will be associated with capturing the knowledge and, in particular, whether it will be feasible to capture the knowledge at all. It will also show up any difficulties that may be experienced in using the system.

On the basis of this prototype, a very quick assessment of the feasibility of a full expert system can be carried out. This would require a more careful statement of the features required of the ultimate system and a brief study of considerations like the technical means for obtaining and structuring the knowledge, any interfaces with existing systems, any real-time links with control systems or fast-changing databases and so on. This will lead to very approximate assessments of the final cost of a project – whether it will be nearer £50,000, £100,000 or £500,000 – and of the benefits. This, together with hands-on experience of the prototype, should make possible a reasonably well-informed decision about whether to take the project any farther.

To gain the maximum benefit from prototyping it is important for the ultimate users to work with the prototype, understand it and criticise it until an acceptable version is produced. If the final system does not satisfy their needs, it will not be used.

DEVELOPING THE SYSTEM

Many companies take one of two approaches if they decide to proceed with a project. One way is to take the conventional data processing approach and prepare a formal system specification. This means defining the business requirements in detail and producing a technical specification which, in effect, calls for a refined feasibility study. The end point of this exercise will be a clearly defined specification and a much more precise idea of what the ultimate system will be like, what it will cost and what advantages will be gained from it.

If a prototype has proved highly successful – and no major difficulties are envisaged in developing the final system – a company may opt a the different approach, continuing development on the basis of the prototype. If the ultimate system is not too large, this can be a very satisfactory way of reaching a workable system quickly and inexpensively. The system may be rather inelegant and contain some weaknesses but it will be in use much sooner and at less expense than one which cannot be started until a formal specification has been prepared.

A 'half-way house' between these two approaches is to discard the prototype and make a fresh start but to proceed without a formal specification. The company could allocate a certain amount of money to the project, in the hope of arriving at a workable product. This is probably the best course to follow if the prototype has given strong grounds for proceeding but where there is a lot of uncertainty about the design of the final system.

Sometimes development of a prototype reveals that a full working system can be achieved using only, say, a rule-based paradigm and that there is already an expert system shell available on which the application can be based. If this turns out to be the case then a full working system of moderate size may be produced at relatively low cost.

SELLING THE IDEA

Alongside the technical assessment of an expert system's feasibility there is an equally important task of 'selling the idea' of an expert system to the people in the company who will be affected by it and whose collaboration is vital. All sorts of fears and antipathies can be roused, even by the name 'expert system' – so it may be wise to avoid using the expression – quite apart from any of the more concrete grounds for opposition.

Within management, generally, there is the task of clarifying exactly what the system will do and removing any false expectations about it. There may well be a comprehensive ignorance about the whole subject, which is not easy for managers to admit, so a general orientation programme may be necessary as well as specific information about the new system and what managers can expect to gain from it.

People who will be closest to the system, either as users or as domain experts whose experience will be required for building the knowledge base, are likely to be highly sensitive about the whole subject. Their collaboration is essential and they must be approached with care and tact.

The first fear is that jobs will be lost, so some reassurance on this count is essential. In fact, very few of the expert systems so far installed around the world have resulted in job losses. The effect, generally, has been to augment the capabilities of expert system users – to free them for other work demanding more skill and judgement, to enhance training programmes and speed up the acquisition of more skill or to enable expansion of activities which would otherwise have been out of the question. Whatever the aim of introducing an expert system, the company's intentions must be made clear.

A particular fear, on the part of experts who are to be 'knowledge engineered', is that they will no longer be needed when their knowledge has been incorporated in the system. With real-life expert systems this is very far from being the case. The present generation of expert systems, at least, can do no more than emulate the more routine aspects of an expert's knowledge. Few expert systems can be left to take decisions on their own, except in the most controlled and restricted of circumstances.

A more cogent argument, which will have to be faced, is that, in building a permanent knowledge base, the expert is doing much more than selling his labour to the company for a salary. He is supplying the company with a capital asset which it will have, in perpetuity, for use, resale, leasing or whatever other purpose the company intends. It is arguable, therefore, and is being argued, that the expert is entitled to special compensation for this acquisition of his expertise.

Almost inevitably, people who are asked to use an expert system will find any excuse to reject it if they have not been introduced to the concept properly. Unfortunately, an expert system is very easily ridiculed because one of its strengths can appear to be a weakness – the fact that it cannot be considered to be 'finished' until a large amount of knowledge has been entered into it. It is very easy to turn this fact on its head saying, "It isn't finished", and to ridicule the system when it offers inept advice. Similar difficulties are encountered with any new computer software but, in expert systems, these are aggravated by the incomplete and evolutionary character of knowledge bases. Unfortunately, there is a tendency for people to think that an 'intelligent system' must be one which can teach itself.

WORKING WITH THE KNOWLEDGE ENGINEER

It is absolutely crucial to achieve a common purpose between the domain expert and the knowledge engineer but there are a number of potential difficulties in that relationship. Knowledge engineers are, typically, young people, not long out of university, articulate and well-versed in their own subjects but probably knowing nothing about the domain to be addressed in an expert system. Domain experts are likely to be mature, highly experienced in their subjects but not necessarily highly articulate and, quite possibly, lacking detailed knowledge of some of the areas for which they are responsible – or, more likely, detail has been overlaid with more general 'rules of thumb' based on a multitude of actual cases. In this sort of situation it is very easy for the expert to be made to look a fool.

A knowledge engineer from PA recalls how one of his early encounters with an expert nearly led to disaster. "I was very young, just out of university, talking to a hardened process man. I needed to get to the bottom of just how a controller worked. It was not enough just to have an informal chat about it – it had to be described very precisely or I could not get the information on to the computer. When I persisted in questioning, the engineer became very angry and walked out. I then realised that he was not able to answer my questions. The controller was a fundamental and quite complicated piece of operating equipment and the engineer would have had to refer to books to describe it in the degree of detail which I needed – a depth of detail which was not necessary for his work. We patched it up eventually and carried on but I learned the lesson that experts can very easily feel threatened. After all, they have been presented by their companies as people who have all the answers and they feel they must uphold their own and the company's prestige."

Having overcome this initial feeling of being threatened, some people develop another fear – that they are telling everything they know and, in consequence, will be worthless to the company. This happens most often with young people who feel that within their knowledge is something others do not know and which they believe gives them an advantage.

After these initial fears, most domain experts develop quite a strong enthusiasm for the task as it progresses. It is also quite common for experts to approach the task with enthusiasm from the outset, with no fears or inhibitions at all.

Unfortunately, though, another attitude often develops after the knowledge engineering task has been progressing for several weeks or, maybe, months – that of sheer boredom. Building a knowledge base is an extremely detailed and painstaking task. Facts, which are obvious to any ordinary human being, have to be spelled out in detail. A process engineer may say, "If the flow of hot oil in this vessel reduces then the temperature of this other vessel will go down." The reason can be quite obvious when one is looking at a drawing of the plant but this is not enough for the knowledge base. One has to specify that the two vessels are connected by a pipe and that there is liquid flowing in the pipe. Usually, it takes some practice before a domain expert learns to think in sufficient detail to be able to build a knowledge base but the ability is soon acquired and experts often come to value the acquisition of this skill. The only serious problem which can arise then, in building a large knowledge base is boredom – and to that there is no simple answer except to avoid sessions that are too long.

Building the knowledge base is the largest and most expensive part of creating an expert system and it is important for a company to realise the scale of commitment it is making. Ordinary computer software, once specified, can, largely, be written outside the company but a knowledge base is essentially something involving the company's own experts. By the very nature of their work, experts are also likely to be very busy people who will find it difficult to spare time for extra-curricular activities like providing a knowledge base. In many cases it is just this sort of pressure on scarce expertise which has made the company decide to adopt an expert system.

It is important to realise that a commitment to creating an expert system is also a commitment to giving the time of experts for building a knowledge base. The scale of that commitment depends, of course, on the size of the knowledge base but building a significant system is rarely likely to occupy an expert for less than three or four months. That period would not be one of full-time activity because, in practice, an individual session cannot run for longer than about two hours – because of the detailed concentration it demands. A typical commitment would be two or three such sessions a week.

The traditional procedure has been for the knowledge engineer to interview the domain expert throughout the period and to build the knowledge base. However, it is argued in this book that it is much preferable – after initial interviews and creation of the knowledge base structure and interface by the knowledge engineer – for the domain expert to work directly on the knowledge base. The knowledge engineer should still be at hand in case of any need to deal with particular difficulties, such as concepts which do not appear to fit into the knowledge base structure. This not only saves time and effort but will also give the domain expert the necessary experience for refining and updating the knowledge base after the expert system has gone into service.

SATISFYING THE END USER

The ultimate user of the expert system may be the domain expert but is more likely to be somebody else – a plant operator, junior radiologist, trainee accountant or a member of the public. Great care is needed when designing the user interface so that it really is helpful to the type of person who will have to work with it and whose background and capabilities may be very different from those of the domain expert.

Design of the dialogue with the user must be carefully pitched at a level appropriate to his or her probable experience. Members of the public may come with questions framed in many different ways and will, quite possibly, need help in clarifying the issues involved. On the other hand, a plant operator, using the system regularly, will require a terse dialogue, reaching a conclusion as quickly as possible. An expert using the system will be able to assess a situation where alternative suggestions are offered, perhaps with probabilities attached to them, whereas an inexperienced user will need to be given a warning message if there is a need to consult an expert or, at least, a clear indication that a suggestion is only tentative. There should always be ample facilities for the system to explain the logical steps and information leading to its recommendations. The way in which these explanations are presented will again depend on the knowledge and experience of the user.

Some computer systems have failed to gain acceptance because they have not taken sufficient account of the way they are going to be used and the environment in which they are to be placed. Expert systems have a potential advantage in that it is easier to tailor them to the specific needs of users but applications in the past have sometimes suffered from too much emphasis on technological merits at the expense of studying how the systems are to be used. User-friendliness can only be achieved by careful attention to detail – it is not automatic.

There is interesting scope for knowledge-based systems acting not as expert systems but as 'intelligent' front-ends to large databases which are accessed by people with differing degrees of experience. By the phrasing of its questions and by the user's answers to them, such a system could gauge how well acquainted the user is with the contents of the database and the methods of using it. A novice user could be led, step by step, through the procedures with ample explanations, while an experienced user could be led quickly to the desired part of the database. A newcomer's growing acquaintance with the procedures could be detected and explanations reduced accordingly.

This is a sophisticated approach, intended for very complicated databases, but a similar way of thinking should inform any user interface of an expert system. Something to be avoided at all costs is the ambiguous probabilistic statement. The sort of nightmare example, which has been seen on occasion in expert systems, is a statement like, "There is a medium probability of x being true (probability = 0.9)". A first reaction would be that a probability of 0.9 is much more than 'medium' but closer study would reveal that the meaning of this is that the system is '0.9 certain' that there is a medium probability. As a general rule, probabilities are best avoided in expert system user interfaces. In most cases they are not necessary and create more confusion than clarity.

Even with the most user-friendly interface, some training of end users will probably be needed to enable them to make the most of the system. This is particularly true if the system is still in the process of refinement. An expert system is, usually, only in a position of 'advisor' to the user and its advice can be accepted or rejected. If advice is rejected, this implies some sort of shortcoming in the system so, if its performance is to improve, there needs to be some means of feedback from the user to ensure better performance next time. The user of a developing system needs to understand that if the system gives bad advice this does not mean it is a bad system. Bad advice means that the system has bad knowledge and bad knowledge can be corrected in the knowledge base to achieve better advice.

If the end user is also a domain expert, he will probably be able to enter the knowledge base and make adjustments to it. If not, it is helpful to incorporate a procedure for logging the users' actions in response to expert system advice. A domain expert can then review user dialogues from time to time and assess the reasons for any rejection of the system's advice, if necessary referring back to the user. In some cases the user is asked to complete a report and to send it to the knowledge engineer if a defect in knowledge is detected. In the ESCORT system for process control, described in the case studies, there is automatic logging of rejected advice, and the process engineer reviewing these rejections has access to the entire instrumentation history of the plant for the period leading up to the rejection.

MAINTAINING THE SYSTEM

As was pointed out in Chapter 2, the point at which a large expert system is handed over to the user is more or less arbitrary. The user will have been involved from an early stage and has probably had the primary responsibility for building the knowledge base. After commissioning, the task of maintaining the knowledge base will continue, though it is to be hoped that the activity will tend to reduce as weaknesses in the knowledge base are detected and removed. However, unless the knowledge base is so small as to be trivial, there will always be some need for an experienced person to maintain it and, where necessary, update it in the light of changed circumstances.

The importance of maintaining the knowledge base is something that cannot be over-emphasised. In the case of databases the importance of maintenance is fully recognised but an out-of-date or erroneous knowledge base can be far more dangerous to its user. Maintaining a large knowledge base, which needs to be frequently updated, is an expensive and time-consuming task for somebody quite senior who is not only an expert in the domain covered but must also be well versed in the structure of the knowledge base and the correct procedures for modifying it. Maintenance, then, will be a continuing commitment and expense for as long as the knowledge base is used, and this cannot be neglected.

IF SOMETHING GOES WRONG

Expert system technology is relatively new and the number of systems earning their keep in industry and commerce is still quite small. Things have been known to go badly wrong, even with conventional software, so is this, perhaps, more likely with an expert system? Discussion of this possibility needs to be divided into two parts.

The basic software of an expert system is its inference engine, together with its various interfaces, work space and so on. If a system has been commissioned from an outside organisation then that organisation may be held responsible if there is any defect in the software. There is no greater likelihood of such errors occurring in an expert system than is the case in any other software. The requirements should be specified, reviewed and agreed to and the software should be developed and tested in exactly the same way, using the same procedures, as with more traditional software.

Our second consideration concerns the knowledge base of an expert system. It is comparable to a database – indeed, it is a sort of database. The structure of a database or a knowledge base, and the way it is accessed by the software, are again the responsibility of the software supplier but the actual content, whether database or knowledge base, is supplied by the user and is the user's responsibility. There is, arguably, a difference where the knowledge base is built by the supplier's knowledge engineer on the basis of interviews with the domain expert but, even here, the system has to be checked and approved by the domain expert who will, ultimately, have to take responsibility for it. This is small comfort to a company which finds that its knowledge base is fundamentally defective – perhaps through lack of capacity, inability to accommodate an important new category of knowledge or because the rule base has become so tangled that it cannot be unravelled. The only answer to these problems is to prevent them – by good prototyping, by carefully specifying the requirements of the system and by using object-oriented programming without too much reliance on rules. On a more optimistic note, though, it is rare for a knowledge base to be so badly structured that it cannot grow into a useful system.

TWO DIFFERENT APPROACHES

This chapter has described some of the most common ways in which companies have launched themselves into expert systems applications but every organisation approaches the subject with different needs. For this reason, we describe two very different examples in the following paragraphs.

Using shells

The first example is from a major food manufacturing company, where the interest in expert systems began with a senior research and development engineer. He had begun to study the changing skill requirements in the company and the opportunities for further computer support. He became interested in expert systems and visited the specialist team at British Petroleum who gave a most impressive demonstration of the speed with which a prototype expert system can be created. At about the same time, the Food Research Association began to study the subject and was considering a project to build a demonstration system.

The engineer saw that there were several potential small applications, in the area of diagnostics and trouble-shooting, which were within the scope of a proprietary expert system shell, allowing systems to be built quickly and without having to acquire artificial intelligence (AI) language expertise. He discussed the possibilities with colleagues in R&D, where a number of people were spending a lot of time in short-term trouble-shooting on manufacturing problems when they should have been free for longer-term creative work.

One of the engineer's colleagues picked up the idea and followed it through with a trouble-shooting application on a production line. The idea was to provide the operator with an on-line service which could advise on the right courses of action in the event of actual or potential faults in the production process. The system began operation in a purely advisory capacity. In the event of a fault developing on the line, the operator would consult the system which would ask him to enter the relevant process conditions – temperature, moisture content and so on, as well as other information. The system would, then, offer a diagnosis of the cause of the trouble and suggestions for putting it right.

As an expert system, it was quite simple but its value was considerable. There were fewer demands on R&D for assistance in shop-floor problems and down-time of the line on the shop-floor was reduced – particularly during night shifts when the operator either had to phone an engineer at home, leaving the line shut down until the engineer arrived in the factory, or, at worst, had to shut down the line for the remainder of the shift.

Having proved the system in an advisory capacity, it became clear that a further step could be taken – to link the line instrumentation directly into the expert system. In this way, the system had a continuous picture of the state of the line and was able to monitor its condition directly, warning the operator of adverse trends before a shut-down became necessary. It was not possible to monitor the line completely automatically because some measurements were outside the scope of process instrumentation and had to be made by the operator before entry into the system. Without this restriction it would have been possible to take the further step of giving the expert system complete control of the process, except where conditions developed which were outside its knowledge or where a shut-down could not be avoided.

Having met with success in one application area the company went on to look at other potential applications. These included providing an intelligent front-end to the company's large library of research and development knowledge on food technology – to avoid needless repetition of established research findings – or matching people's skills and their training and development programmes to the expected range of future job requirements.

If an expert system is seen to work in one key area of a company, people will be quick to see opportunities for extending its scope into other, related areas or for implementing new systems in analogous situations.

Starting from the ground up

Travel agents, Thomas Cook, entered expert system applications in a strongly do-it-yourself style in 1982. Brian Fearns, at that time the group's manager of technology planning and research, had his interest in the subject raised by the crop of conferences on what was, then, a very new subject. He set up a three-week fact-finding tour of the USA, spending time with three leading companies which were experienced in expert systems and in natural language processing, a parallel interest. It was a highly intensive experience during which Fearns had to get to grips with the jargon and learn the fundamentals of the programming languages Lisp and Prolog and the AI tool-kit KEE.

On his return to the UK, he gave about 20 presentations to executives and staff, explaining what expert systems were, how they differed from natural language processing and how these two AI technologies might be applied within Thomas Cook. Next, he set out to find suitable domains for experimental applications, soon reaching the conclusion that it would not be easy to set up a small model of a natural language processing environment and that it would be too risky to go for a full-scale project.

On expert systems he was more successful. The key to success with expert systems, Fearns believes, is finding a small application with clearly defined boundaries but which contains all the functionality that would be required in a large-scale application with a much broader domain.

Together with his colleagues, and in particular with Bob Ruckwood who is, today, technology consultant to the group, Fearns decided that an appropriate subject for an expert system would be a facility to help business travellers create itineraries where they have to optimise on a number of things – fixed or slightly movable start and finish dates for a tour, some fixed appointments, some movable appointments, some desirable but not essential visits and some flexibility in the places to be visited and the sequence of events, all with minimum lost time and, maybe, other requirements such as minimum cost or first-class travel and accommodation.

A full-scale expert system would need to draw on the vast databases of airline flights and reservations as well as hotels and rail and other services. Developing such a system would be a very large undertaking indeed, so something smaller was needed – something which would require resolution of all the same problems but on a much smaller scale.

After a search, involving sessions with about 20 people in Thomas Cook who were experts in different forms of travel, the ideal model was found in Railways of Australia, a self-contained travel service for which Thomas Cook was the general sales agent in the UK and, so, handled all UK bookings. There was also an expert, Derek Townsend, who had an intimate knowledge of every aspect of rail travel in Australia and was approaching retirement age.

The pilot expert system on Railways of Australia was written in Prolog, without the aid of a shell or tool-kit, in collaboration with the software company, Expert Systems International. It was based on an IBM PC/AT, with a colour monitor, and, because it had to be used during telephone conversations with travel agents, it was used entirely through a graphic interface driven by a light pen.

The basic display was of a map of Australia, indicating states and major towns. Using the light pen, more detailed maps could be called up, showing towns and stations, for identifying an itinerary. Across the top of the screen were icons – illustrating things like a calendar for the date, a train for timetable information and a ticket – which could be pointed to by the light pen to associate dates, times, fares and so on with the prospective itinerary.

So, the user was able to plan a route while on the telephone to the travel agent, taking into account restraints on time available, the number of nights on and off the train, travel through different time zones, allowances for connections between trains and so on. The system could then produce a printed itinerary containing all the recommendations and background information.

As the system was able to take into account not only the complete timetable but also information like the availability of hotels, tourist attractions and so on, it could produce much more practical itineraries than a non-expert person would be likely to work out with a train timetable and a batch of handbooks – and in very much less time.

The system was eventually withdrawn from use, mainly because of maintenance costs. Also, the timetable information from Australia was not available in an electronic form, so major updates in the timetable had to be entered manually, at great expense. However, a great deal was learned from the exercise which is helping to guide further work by Thomas Cook.

Some of the lessons from this and other knowledge-based system activities were pointed out recently by Ruckwood:

- The system did many clever things but it would have been much more valuable if it had been able to do some simple things, like sending a telex and printing a ticket.
- Knowledge in databases and reference books is passive – somebody has to dig it out before it can become useful. A knowledge-based system can present such information to the user as it is needed, so that it becomes active knowledge. For example, airline manuals contain information about how the airline defines children for ticket-charging purposes and about what price reductions are available for children. If the information were made active in a knowledge base, it would be very much easier to recommend to a customer which airline to use with a child of, say, 13½ years of age.
- A knowledge-based system does not have to be complicated to be valuable. In a typical office, most people work satisfactorily. Some are very good and some are poor. If a knowledge-based system can simply eliminate poor performance it can help greatly in maintaining quality and corporate image.
- Maintenance of a complex expert system is a significant task which continues as long as the system is required. Domain experts continue to play an important role in monitoring, updating,

validating and enhancing the system.
- The larger the system, the more important hardware performance becomes.

SUMMARY

- The person spearheading the investigation of expert systems should be an enthusiast, computer literate and, preferably, from the area of the company most likely to benefit.
- Expect to see an example of a similar application if a software company or consultant is commissioned to develop a system.
- Prototyping the proposed system is a low-cost way of gaining some understanding of how it will function.
- The most rigorous starting point for further development would be a system specification.
- If the system is not large and if the prototype is very successful, it may be less expensive to continue development from the prototype.
- Where the prototype gives strong grounds for proceeding but where further development will introduce unknown elements, it may be best to assign a fixed sum for that development.
- Selling the advantages of an expert system to all concerned in the organisation is as important as ensuring its technical and economic feasibility.
- It is necessary to address the fear, of users and domain experts, that they will no longer be needed.
- A good working relationship between the knowledge engineer and the domain expert is absolutely crucial.
- It must be accepted, in launching the project, that building an expert system will make heavy demands on the time of domain experts – who are already under pressure.
- Adequate feedback is needed from end user to domain expert to ensure the continuous improvement of the knowledge base.
- In the event of shortcomings in the system, the developer may be held responsible for defects in the software but the main responsibility for the knowledge base is, inevitably, with the user organisation.
- Ways of getting started in expert systems will differ according to the nature and structure of the organisation and the most likely application areas.

5 THE FUTURE OF
EXPERT SYSTEMS

AT the beginning of 1990 the signs were that the biggest short-term growth in knowledge-based systems would be in those smaller applications, based on the latest generation of more powerful expert system shells. Over the next few years, however, large systems should come into service much more, as their extensive knowledge bases are built and verified.

Several factors point to a healthy growth in expert system applications during the 1990s:

- Recognition of need by potential users.
- Lower costs and more power in hardware and software.
- Developments in technology.
- Improved quality assurance.
- Wider dissemination of experience with expert systems.

These factors are discussed further in the following paragraphs.

RECOGNITION OF NEED

As companies and organisations become aware that knowledge, as distinct from data, can be stored, accumulated, accessed, manipulated and used to provide advice and help in complex tasks, the opportunities for applying knowledge-based systems will be increasingly recognised.

Expert systems carry further a trend which began with the industrial revolution and the mechanisation followed by the automation of manual skills. During the past twenty years or so the information technology revolution has made great progress in the automation of routine clerical work but, as yet, there has been little impact on decision-making activities which, by comparison, are highly labour-intensive.

At the same time, the supply of information and advice is becoming increasingly important, and not only in the service industries which form a growing sector of the economy. All industries are finding the need to provide more information for customers and clients. More complex equipment requires more detailed operating instructions and better maintenance or trouble-shooting information which can be accessed more quickly and easily.

Engineering and manufacturing functions in industry are being required to take more factors into account when making decisions. Design engineers, for example, are expected to consider ease and cost of production and assembly, suitability of new materials, adhesives and manufacturing techniques, as well as the consequences of operation under widely varying ambient conditions. Each consideration may have to take account of wide expertise in technologies outside the experience of the design engineer. The incorporation of such knowledge, in expert systems which can be accessed easily by the engineer, can greatly enhance the effectiveness of design work.

Demographic factors are intensifying the need to capture and preserve expertise. An increasing proportion of the population, both in the UK and in other major countries, is reaching retirement age and there are fewer young people coming into employment. Hence, there is often nobody available to whom expertise can be passed on and, certainly there are fewer people willing to dedicate years of their lives to acquiring the expertise achieved with difficulty by their elders – not least because changing technologies bring changing skill requirements.

In some application areas, knowledge-based systems are coming along just in time to assist with a mass of decision making that is approaching the limit of capability for human expertise. This is true, for example, in the control of major process plants and with large telecommunications systems.

HARDWARE AND SOFTWARE DEVELOPMENTS

The rapid rise in computing power and simultaneous fall in computing costs, which are influencing the whole field of computer applications, are also having an effect on expert systems, with hardware and software developments going hand in hand.

Development of large knowledge-based systems is commonly carried out at powerful workstations using special tool-kit software, and several things are happening in this area. Workstations are becoming faster in use and less expensive, making them more attractive to prospective users. The latest generation of personal computers is more powerful, with more speed, memory capacity and higher resolution screen displays, and some of the major tool-kits now have versions capable of being run on personal computers.

What is true for expert system development is also true for applications. It is now realistic to think of the most sophisticated personal computers, with powerful operating systems and large memory capacity, as being quite suitable for running many real-time on-line applications.

At the same time, expert system shells are going up-market. Some of them now have versions for use on various makes of workstations and a few have versions for development and implementation on minicomputers and mainframes. In the past there has been a fairly well-defined gap between tool-kits and shells but the middle ground is now being filled from both sides. The most sophisticated products from companies supplying shells now incorporate such refinements as object-oriented programming, use of frames and inheritance, mathematical modelling of processes, handling of uncertainty and so on.

TECHNICAL TRENDS

The most time-consuming and costly part of creating an expert system is building the knowledge base, and efforts are being made to find ways of reducing the labour required for this task. The case has already been argued for the approach which tries to minimise the need for the knowledge engineer by creating a knowledge interface which the domain expert can use directly.

Rule induction

Mention was made in Chapter 3 of an approach to automating the creation of a knowledge base. This is now available with some expert system shells, using a family of techniques employing the principle of induction – of inferring a general rule from a number of particular instances. The method is to present the system with a number of instances of questions with answers which would be supplied by an expert. The system then analyses these questions and answers and automatically produces a set of rules which can account for the particular linkages of questions and answers.

The technique by-passes all the hard work of establishing a reliable set of rules by knowledge engineering and, for a small system, it can be quite practical. It is certainly a useful way of attracting interest in expert systems. However, where larger numbers of examples have to be instanced, to cover the scope of the expert system, the time required to generate the automatic rules increases considerably, and the induced rules increase in complexity.

It may be that future developments will increase the size of an expert system which can be generated by induced rules but there is an inherent difficulty in that the rules generated by this method make no sense at all to an ordinary expert. It is possible to verify that the system always gives the 'right' answer to any set of questions but it is not easy to enter the system and check or modify the logical structure of the rules generated. Also, the system cannot, by itself, exhibit 'intelligence' in the ordering of its questions. All questions are treated as though of equal importance and the interview with the user cannot be structured to emphasise priority questions or follow the natural sequence of activities in, say, fault diagnosis on a piece of equipment, for example dealing first with matters which can be checked easily before going on to questions involving disassembly or bringing in special equipment.

Despite these difficulties, people who have used this method claim that it can serve as the first step in developing a larger expert system and that it can check whether any questions are redundant or if there are not enough questions to allow reliable decisions to be reached. Induction is currently available with at least two different expert system shells and it is possible that ways may be found of integrating induction more effectively with other methods of developing knowledge-based systems.

Genetic algorithms

Another approach, showing signs of promise, is one based on Darwin's principles of mutation and natural selection. In simple terms, an expert system is given a 'random knowledge generator' which will corrupt or 'mutate' its existing knowledge. The system also has another knowledge base which is designed to test the mutated knowledge base for validity, assigning a strength of validity to it. If the strength is above a predetermined level, the mutated knowledge is retained and becomes the 'parent' of further mutations, otherwise it is discarded.

In this way, a number of mutated knowledge bases are accumulated and the system continues to test these. If, after, say, ten problems, a particular piece of mutated knowledge is found to be consistently reliable, the system starts to incorporate it in the original knowledge base so that it becomes part of the reasoning equipment of the system. By the end of some months of such mutation, natural selection and incorporation of the 'fittest' mutants, the system will consist very largely of mutated knowledge and might be said to have been learning automatically.

PA is one of the organisations looking very seriously at genetically mutating algorithms and hopes to have factory process planning systems based on them before the end of 1990. In such a case, the method involves a simulation of the operation of a medium-size batch production factory. Random mutations in the process plan are tested for efficiency and 'natural selection' will allow the evolution of a better system. Other potential application areas are seen as finance and process plant control.

Neural networks

A different model from the process of evolution is the working of the human brain itself. It would be a wild overstatement to say that neural networks operate in the same way as the human brain but they are designed to function in a similar way to the human nervous system. Like the nervous system, a neural network consists of a number of electronic 'neurons' connected together in a network, with inputs and outputs. When inputs to a 'neuron' exceed a certain level it 'fires' and its output ripples through the network, producing a particular output to the external world.

A neural network can incorporate some 'learning' capability and demonstrate some expert system characteristics but it is strongly dependent on its hard wiring and research in this area is still at a very early stage.

Parallel processing

Computers built with transputers and other parallel processing devices, and software which can take advantage of them, will help to make possible the introduction of larger knowledge-based systems. One particular approach, which is not new but whose implementation could be hastened by the availability of parallel processing systems, is known as the 'blackboard architecture'. Much of the past interest in this subject has come from military requirements.

A 'blackboard system' can be pictured as a group of experts, each knowing different aspects of a subject, gathered around a blackboard trying to assess a situation – such as whether an approaching aircraft is friend or foe. One expert, say on radar, will make a judgement based on available information and expertise and write it on the blackboard, together with the reasoning behind that judgement. Taking account of this new information, another expert will add an assessment based on a different type of expertise – perhaps of aircraft performance. In this way, different types of expertise can be brought together and modified in the light of other expertise and of growing factual information.

Parallel processing will make it easier for a number of expert systems to work in parallel on the same knowledge base and to interact with each other at a speed which will be practical in real situations.

APPLICATION TRENDS

As yet, the rate of introduction of large-scale expert systems has been disappointing – mainly because the cost of investment in a large system is high as is the risk of ending up with something which is not really cost effective, even though the rewards from a successful investment can be very large. It is also true that there is a shortage of people and organisations with sufficient knowledge and experience to take on a large project with a reasonable expectation of success. These hindrances will disappear over the next few years but, meanwhile, it is expected that there will be a rapid growth in smaller systems based on proprietary expert system shells.

Another likely growth area will be the introduction of 'intelligent front-ends' for large databases. Knowledge-based systems development is leading to the creation of user interfaces which are much more sensitive to the needs of the user – in stark contrast to most present-day computer interfaces which force the user to conform to the rigid requirements of a computer program. As access to large company and public databases becomes more widely available, it will be increasingly important to have, between the user and the massive database, a system which can respond to different levels of user skill and knowledge and which, by means of dialogue, can ascertain the user's real requirements and carry out database searches on his or her behalf. So, a relatively small expert system and knowledge base can greatly simplify the use of a large database.

Hypertext is one of the newer concepts which can give added usefulness to knowledge-based front-ends. Whereas ordinary textual material is read serially from beginning to end, hypertext allows the important words and phrases in a text to be linked, in a network, to each other and to further material. This further material can explain or supply additional matter – as text, graphical or tabulated material, drawings, photographs and so on – to help in the understanding and use of the basic text. It is possible, if required, to go even further and link the original text to colour video, sound, animation and other information aids. Instead of simply reading the supplied text, the user is able to browse, pursuing particular lines of interest in as much depth as necessary. An example of such an approach, supporting a diagnostic expert system, is given in the IBM case study in the next section. Hypertext can be used with expert systems to provide a valuable training aid and some work is now in progress to integrate hypertext and expert systems more closely. This will mean that the hypertext becomes not simply a passive network of relationships in which the user can easily become lost but that it can actively assist the user in navigating through a large mass of information.

Looking at trends from another point of view, what we shall be seeing increasingly during the next few years is knowledge-based systems embedded in more conventional software, so that many existing traditional software systems will acquire some degree of 'intelligence' in their interactions with users. It has also been suggested elsewhere in this book that programming methods, like object-oriented programming, which have developed in the artificial intelligence community and been applied most effectively in knowledge-based systems, will increasingly become fundamental tools in all types of software development.

QUALITY ASSURANCE

As expert systems are highly complex pieces of software which may contain elements of probability and expert judgement, it is more, not less, necessary to ensure that good prototyping practice is followed and that prototypes are properly validated and verified, despite the difficulties involved.

Guidelines on the quality assurance of expert systems have been published by the Computing Services Association, emphasising the importance of disciplined and well-documented prototyping of expert systems. The association proposes a prototyping life cycle in three basic stages – definition, construction and evaluation – which, in an iterative prototyping activity, would follow on from each other, cyclically. For an operational system, production of an agreed prototype would be followed by requirements definition, design, implementation and integration – including testing.

The association underlines the need for quality assurance standards to be developed to cover expert systems development and prototyping, and it outlines the procedures that should be followed and documentation which should be produced in support of an expert system project. The essential point of the association's recommendations is that expert systems development should follow the same general principles as any other software systems development. There is no reason for by-passing good software development practice simply because expert systems have special features.

Validation (testing that the expert system gives the same answers to questions as would an expert) and verification (testing that the knowledge base is logically sound and complete) are acknowledged by the association to be difficult because of the nature of the knowledge and the very large number of possible cases to be tested. However, the association concludes that more, not less, work is required on testing of expert systems software.

In the case of verification of logical consistency and completeness, some degree of automation is possible. Various tests exist for redundancy, circularity, missing rules and other logical defects in the knowledge base and further work is in progress in this area.

WIDER EXPERTISE

Perhaps the most important factor leading to the future growth of expert systems will be the growing number of people with experience in developing and implementing such systems. Today's knowledge engineers, who are the essential agents in getting expert systems up and running, have come from a variety of academic disciplines – artificial intelligence, computing science, psychology and linguistics as well as from more conventional science, technology and business administration backgrounds. As the technology becomes more widespread it can expect to find its way into undergraduate studies as well as being covered increasingly in special short courses.

A very useful addition to many undergraduate studies, or even at secondary education level, would be an introduction to logical analysis – to give people a way of thinking that enables them to express knowledge in terms of rules. This would make it much easier for people, as they gain expertise, to take advantage of the facilities offered by knowledge-based systems.

This is by no means a fanciful idea – many schoolchildren today have acquired skills in using the more conventional computing languages and a study of logic would be educationally much more valuable.

SECTION 2

CASE STUDIES

CASE STUDIES
INTRODUCTION

THE ten case studies that follow cover a wide variety of expert systems applications, in terms of size, type of industry and application, and method of development. They have been chosen to give some idea of the different ways in which organisations have approached expert systems applications.

Largest of the systems described here is the one now going into service at the BP Chemicals butadiene plant at Grangemouth in Scotland. Developed by PA Consulting Group, it is believed to be the largest expert system of its type in Europe and is expected to be a forerunner of still larger systems in more complex process plants. It is described here in some detail to give an indication of the work involved in building a large expert system.

A company which started in quite a small way, using the programming language Prolog, but which has gone on to develop a variety of successful systems, is Lucas Engineering and Systems, an organisation which acts primarily in a consultancy role within the Lucas Group but which is now beginning to offer some of its expert systems on the open market.

Starting from a specific technical sales problem, John Crane Seals has developed a unique system solution, working first with a system using Prolog and then graduating to a low-cost tool-kit.

A very different entry route was adopted by Clarks Shoes, where a general awareness of the need to take on board the latest ideas in information technology led to the sponsoring of one of its own employees through university. This employee built an expert system prototype for his PhD thesis and is now following through a complex scheduling application.

Fault diagnosis is one of the most frequently adopted applications for small expert systems but the system developed by IBM at Greenock is very different – in size, complexity, profitability and in the way it tackles the extremely difficult task of fault diagnosis on a rapidly changing product. The system was developed by IBM using a major tool-kit and Lisp machine.

Not general enough to be called a shell, but not an entirely bespoke development for every application, is ISSUE, originally developed by PA Consulting Group for one client's application but in a format which has been found adaptable to many other situations, particularly financial applications.

One of the first successful large expert systems in the world was XCON, developed for Digital Equipment Corporation in the USA, for configuration of computer hardware. The latest version of the system, with some new variations, is still very much in service. It has been extensively described at conferences and in publications but a brief summary of it is included in this section.

American Express went to Symbolics, an expert system hardware and software supplier, for a system to help cope with the enormous task of evaluating and authorising high-value purchases using the company's charge cards – shopkeepers phone American Express for confirmation that a card-holder can make say, a $500 dollar purchase and they need an almost instant answer.

One way of obtaining an almost bespoke expert system, without all the expense and risk of funding it oneself, is to join a club project. Two such projects are described here:

● The first is a large project, run by the Harwell Laboratory in association with the National Physical Laboratory, to produce a linked family of expert systems on corrosion. Due for completion in 1990, the project covers many aspects of corrosion protection and prevention in many different environments and with different combinations of materials. This report also describes other consultancy work in progress at Harwell.

- The other club project is in a totally different application area – that of procurement planning and control for very large projects. There is an obvious military interest in the subject but other members of this club include Midland Bank and the National Health Service. Contractor to the project is PA Consulting Group and it is partly public-funded, by the Department of Trade and Industry, as a post-Alvey project.

BP CHEMICALS GRANGEMOUTH – A LARGE PROCESS CONTROL EXPERT SYSTEM

BP Chemicals is currently (1990) completing the installation of what is believed to be the largest real-time expert system in Europe, at its Grangemouth butadiene manufacturing plant in Scotland. The system, known as ESCORT, can handle data from 7,000 process measurement points while supervising up to 1,000 control loops and can be used not only to advise operators on preventive and corrective action but also, where appropriate, to deal with certain control functions automatically.

According to John Morse, project director of Grangemouth development projects for BP Chemicals, the implications of the new system for plant management are considerable. On a day-to-day basis, operational advice which it provides is expected to save the company money, by improving production efficiency and reliability. On some plants ESCORT should pay for all its implementation costs within a year of start-up. The early warning and fault recovery functions the system provides, however, are also a safeguard against the threat of large-scale operational crises and the risk of human error.

ESCORT, which stands for Expert System for Complex Operations in Real Time, was developed by PA Consulting Group specifically for applications of this type. In its plant management version, the ESCORT software itself is an expert system shell – albeit a very large one, with interfaces to the plant instrumentation data, to the plant operators and to the process engineers who build and maintain the knowledge base. It is applicable to any large process plant such as an oil production platform or refinery or a chemical plant.

The system is able to monitor a large number of process measurements and continually make intelligent hypotheses about what is happening, so that it can present to the operator a summary account of the state of the plant, together with suggestions for corrective action where necessary.

This is the capability which is being provided by the ESCORT system at Grangemouth. In addition, the system is expected to provide early warning of potential problems, before they would normally become apparent to the operators, and to generate remedial advice allowing the operators to take preventive action.

The idea for the project began in 1984 when Royston Sargeant, of PA, produced a demonstration set-up for the oil and gas industry to show how an expert system could help overcome some serious problems that were being encountered in large process plants. These problems focus on the fact that very large amounts of information are being made available to the operators in the control rooms of such plants. The information may come in the form of instrument dials, computer screen displays, warning lights, audible warnings and so on. Some of the information is important, some less so. Some changes in the plant will cause several warnings to be presented to the operator simultaneously or in close succession.

With so much information being presented, it sometimes becomes difficult for the operators to assess what is actually happening in the plant and to take the appropriate action. There may be three or four operators in the control room but this problem of 'cognitive overload' is not solved by increasing the number of people because they have to communicate with each other and agree in their interpretations of events.

In the past few years there have been some grim reminders of the dangers associated with cognitive overload – one need only name the Three Mile Island generating station. On the other hand, the wealth of information now made available can, if used properly, add greatly to the efficient running of a plant.

PA's original suggestion met with a cautious response from the industry, where unexpected problems had been created by previous rounds of high technology investment in process control systems. However, this did not deter PA from designing and building a realistic prototype and demonstration system, which was shown publicly in 1985. A simulation was created, on a PDP11 computer, of an offshore production platform – rather like an arcade game in which an operator could attempt to maintain control while a supervisor injected a variety of difficult situations into the plant. The simulation and the problems were realistic and experienced operators had difficulty in preventing the plant from shutting itself down.

The prototype expert system was built, running on a Xerox 1108 workstation which received only the same data as were presented to the operator. From this information it built hypotheses about what was happening in the plant and presented the root problems, in order of priority, to the operator. The improvement in the operator's performance with this additional knowledge was dramatic and, in 1986, PA won funding from a number of major organisations for full feasibility studies. Then, in 1987, BP requested full specifications and a start on a full-scale implementation for Grangemouth.

The main requirements influencing the design of ESCORT were:

- The system must provide advice on plant problems within a few seconds (which is a typical requirement of conventional process control systems).
- The advice must indicate both the causes of a problem and the importance of it relative to other existing problems.
- The system should provide advice on control and instrumentation problems, such as transmitter failures and processing difficulties, and unpredicted combinations of problems.
- The operator must always remain in control of the system, not the other way round.
- The system, as delivered, must be capable of installation without modification to the process plant so it can only have access to the same data as the process control computers.
- Overall, there must be net benefits to the operator of using rather than ignoring ESCORT.

At Grangemouth, on the butadiene plant, there is a process control computer and this is accessed by a VAX gateway computer to supply continuous information to the expert system computer about the state of the plant (see Fig. 1). Results of the expert system's analysis of the

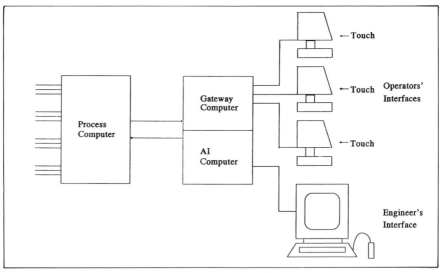

Fig. 1. Block diagram of ESCORT system structure

situation are presented to the operators on touch-sensitive colour screens. A separate terminal, with a large high-resolution display screen, allows process engineers to obtain access to the system's knowledge base. A typical operator's display is shown in Fig. 2.

PA	Refresh 13:17		**ESCORT**		Action!		⌃

Causes

XP-8-A	PUMP	CAVITATING	F1019 Output-Value Too-Low
F1007	OUTPUT-VALVE	LOW	
LV018	VALVE POSITION	STUCK-CLOSED	L1012 Output-Value Too-High
L1018	LEVEL-INDICATOR	FAULTY	

text continues

Action

	old value	new value	mode	LAHH045 Alarm On
1. FC014 SET-POINT	12.0	24.0	AUTO	
2. FV17 VALVE-POS	CHECK		OPERATOR	
3. PUMP X-P-8A	CHECK		OPERATOR	T1183 Output-Value Low
4. LC018 SET-POINT	52.0	73.0	PERMIT	

Symptoms

F1019	OUTPUT-VALUE	TOO-LOW	
L1018	LO-ALARM	STATUS-ON	
L1018	OUTPUT-VALUE	TOO-LOW	
F1015	OUTPUT-VALUE	LOW	

text continues

Accept	Reject	Why	More	Help	⌄

Fig. 2. Operator's touch sensitive screen interface

The operator's display has, on its right-hand side, a 'priority ladder' of up to six problems occurring on the plant, with the most urgent at the top. By touching any of the six boxes on the screen, the operator can obtain a more detailed explanation of each of these problems, with an indication of the symptoms, advice on the action to be taken, and a list of any alarms that may be running as a result of the problem. If more than six problem conditions are active at once, they are placed on a ladder 30 steps long and, as their relative priorities change, the order of the entries on the ladder changes. The operator can always view a section of the ladder six steps long.

The default situation is that the main area of the screen is displaying advice and information on the plant problem heading the priority ladder. However, the operator may be consulting the system on any of the other problems and, in any case, priorities may change at any time. At the top of the screen, therefore, is an 'alert bar' which is coloured according to the urgency of the problem at the top of the priority ladder. A green status bar indicates that there are no current problems or that those that exist have no major detrimental effect. If the bar changes to yellow it means that there are problems but that the highest priority problem, although significant, does not require immediate attention. If the alert bar is red it indicates that the problem should be attended to immediately.

Along the bottom of the screen is another row of touch 'buttons'. Pressing 'Why' brings on to the screen an explanation of the reasoning behind the diagnosis of the problem currently displayed. Other buttons allow the operator to select different operating regimes, input information to ESCORT directly, inhibit or enable control actions and so on.

STRUCTURE OF THE SYSTEM

Time is critically important in the running of ESCORT and has necessitated its structuring as five interconnected expert systems and a knowledge base with several elements. The systems work together to provide real-time advice and information. Their relationship is shown in Fig. 3. Information, coming from the plant via the gateway computer, is detected in the first stage system and unimportant information is filtered out. Anything which may call for some action is recognised and passed to the next stage as a list of events. This list includes not only alarm signals from the plant but also other combinations of events which could lead to alarms or other critical situations.

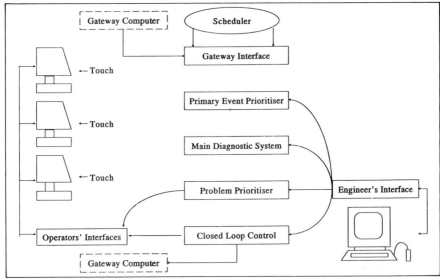

Fig. 3. Five expert systems co-operate and use a knowledge base with several elements

Next, this list of events is rearranged on the basis of relative importance, for example in relation to the different areas of the plant and the events within them. This is a fairly crude sorting but it eases the load on subsequent stages.

The prioritised list is then analysed by the main diagnostic system which is the largest module in the system. It has two tasks:

- To diagnose the underlying problem that caused a new event.
- To keep current problems up to date.

This module has access to all the process plant data available to the operator and makes full use of the plant representation knowledge and rules in the knowledge base to reach its diagnoses.

Finally, these diagnoses of problems are arranged in order of importance, in terms of maintaining plant production and avoiding shut-down, and it is this prioritisation which is used to construct the priority ladder on the operator's screen display, together with the information about the underlying cause of the problem and recommended action.

Supervising all these activities is a knowledge-based scheduler system which determines which activities to perform next, taking into account what new events have occurred, the state of diagnosis of current problems and commands issued by the operator.

ELEMENTS OF THE KNOWLEDGE BASE

The knowledge used by ESCORT is of two main types, as shown in Fig. 4. An essential requirement for a process plant system is a representation of the plant itself, showing how its parts interrelate. Included in the representation is the piping and instrumentation (P&I) diagram, part of which is shown in the engineer's interface screen Fig. 5. The diagram gives a computer representation of the relationships between vessels, pipes, valves and so on, together with information on the direction of flow, the contents of vessels, the code references of instruments and other details – all in a format which can be readily understood by the process engineer.

Also required in the plant representation are definitions of the various components of the plant and how they relate to each other in ways other than their physical relationship shown in the P&I diagram. At the left of Fig. 5 is part of a class inheritance lattice covering analogue sensors. As explained in Chapter 2, each class item in the lattice is held in the knowledge base as an 'object' containing knowledge about it, and it also 'inherits' knowledge from its 'parent' class, to the left of it. At the far right of the full diagram are all the individual sensors from which information is collected.

The full description of the plant involves a number of such relationships, described in such terms as 'is-a-part-of', 'has-parts', 'is-a-kind-of', 'is-an-input-to', 'is-an-output-of', and so on.

The other means of expressing knowledge in ESCORT is through rules. These are not held in a single large list but are divided up according to their function and the part of the system to which they relate. There are rules specific to each of the subsidiary expert systems – event detection rules, event prioritisation rules, problem prioritisation rules and scheduling rules.

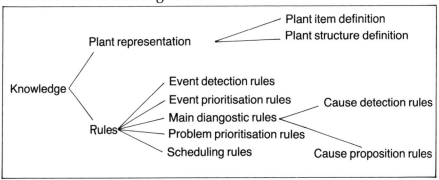

Fig. 4. Categories of knowledge used by ESCORT

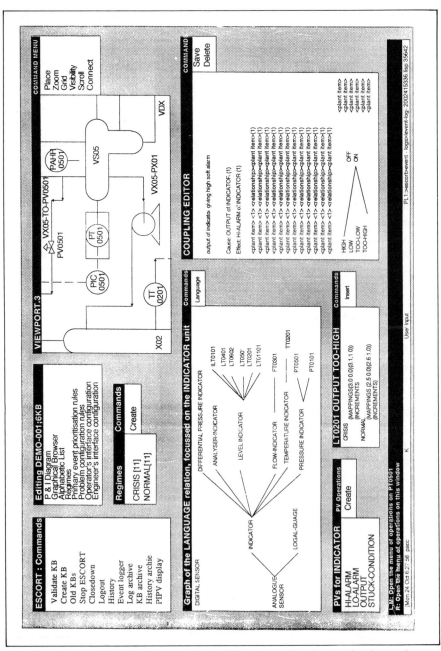

Fig. 5. Engineer's interface provides a full range of tools on a high resolution monochrome display

The rules in the main diagnostic system are attached to the 'objects' to which they relate and are only called upon as situations arise which may require them. In consequence, an individual event in the plant will generally result in the 'firing' of not more than 1% of the rules in the knowledge base. The inheritance structure of the knowledge base minimises the number of rules that need to be entered and ensures that certain rules and rule sets are called upon frequently. For example, a set of rules for determining if a control valve might be stuck will be the same for every control valve in the plant and will be called every time an event requires the checking of a control valve. In addition, there are rules that are specific to a particular piece of plant or a particular situation but these are kept to as few as possible.

ESCORT statements are always in the form of 'triples', sets of three words like 'liquid level high' or 'indicator output too-low' and these can be combined to create rules known as 'causal couplings', invoking an effect, a cause and the link between cause and effect. For example:

> Effect: level-transmitter reading high
> Cause: vessel-liquid level high
> Links: level-transmitter measures vessel-liquid

which means, 'if a level-transmitter is reading high, then one possible cause is that the liquid it is measuring has a high level'.

BUILDING HYPOTHESES

The task of the diagnostic system is to analyse events as they are presented to it and to search for causes, which it passes to the prioritisation system for presentation to the operator. The system's interpretation of what is happening is represented by a hypothesis network in which each hypothesis represents some assertion, with an assessment of its truth or falsity on a scale of 0 to 1.

As each piece of information comes in from the plant it is presented to the plant representation and the causal couplings in order to create a hypothesis about it. Each element used in building the hypothesis can be represented by the boxes in a network, like that shown in Fig. 6. Each hypothesis is tested, if possible. If it cannot be tested directly, it is possible to arrive at a verdict on it from other hypotheses by a process known as 'truth propagation'. Every tested hypothesis has a strength value assigned to it, which depends on its relationship to other tested hypotheses and is obtained by the automatic process of

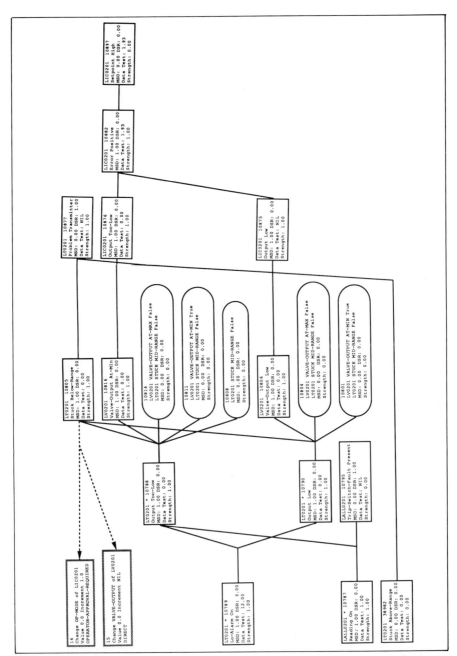

Fig. 6. Hypothesis network represents the system's current view of what is happening

'negotiation and arbitration'.

In a real-time situation, information is coming in all the time and hypotheses change and develop. The current results of hypotheses are continually passed to the prioritising system for presentation to the operator.

CREATING THE KNOWLEDGE BASE

Building the knowledge base has been mainly the task of BP's own process engineers. This has been made possible by the creation, within ESCORT, of an engineer's interface which runs on a Symbolics workstation. The process engineer does not work with programming languages directly. The interface, of which a typical display is shown in Fig. 5, makes extensive use of 'windowing' to allow the engineer to enter and test knowledge in a way which accords with the engineer's natural method of working. Relationships between elements in the plant are presented in the form of a P&I diagram, which can be altered and updated directly by the engineer. Relationships such as 'is-a-type-of' are presented in tree structures, as at the left of Fig. 5 and in Fig. 7. An individual item can be identified from a diagram, using a 'mouse' at the terminal, and the knowledge, contained in the frame/object for that item, presented in another window on the screen. Pointing with the mouse at an individual item within the frame will bring up a further window which will allow information to be entered in simple English, without the complicated system of brackets and other symbols demanded by the underlying Lisp language.

The same interface is being used by engineers to test the whole system and will be used, when ESCORT is fully operational at Grangemouth, to carry on the maturation of the knowledge base as further experience is gained with it under practical operating conditions.

TESTING THE SYSTEM

A large expert system like ESCORT requires extensive testing, both of the system software and of the knowledge base for the particular application. It is important to distinguish these two parts of the system. PA is responsible for the software but BP is responsible for the specific application knowledge.

What PA did to exercise and test the ESCORT software was to adopt

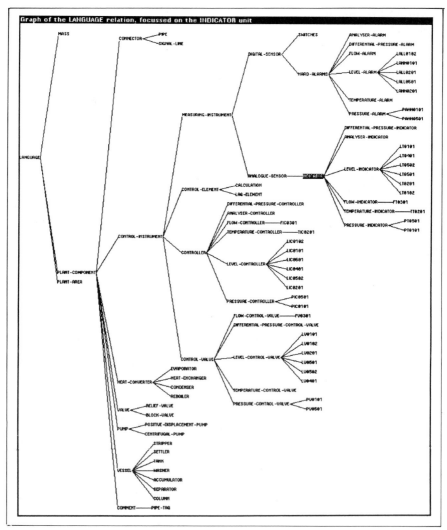

Fig. 7. Relationships, such as 'is-a-type-of', are represented in tree structures.

a small process simulation against which it could be run. The simulation had to be large enough to be representative of reasonably complex process phenomena. On the other hand, the size had to be limited because it was essential that reasonably competent process engineers should be able to anticipate and predict all the different ways in which the variables in the simulation might interact, so that they could develop essentially 'perfect' knowledge bases. The simulation adopted for testing ESCORT was one for a hypothetical natural gas liquid (NGL) plant which had been in use for four years and was well understood.

This simulation formed the knowledge base for testing the ability of ESCORT to create valid hypotheses in a wide variety of situations. In some cases it was found that what appeared to be defects in ESCORT's inference engine were, in fact, errors in the process simulation, even though it had been running for four years. The software was tested module by module and as a complete system until PA was confident that both the core software and the NGL simulation were free from errors. At the end of this exercise the company was in possession not only of tested core software but also of a reliable plant simulation which could be used as a test bed for any future enhancements of the expert system. The core software may be considered to provide an expert system with general knowledge about process control – having a 'degree' in control engineering but no specific application knowledge.

The primary knowledge base for the Grangemouth installation represents something like 30 man-weeks of work and testing it was a separate, very large task which had to be carried out, as far as possible, before the system was installed in the plant. With something like 3,000 separate data inputs coming from the process computer, it was no use simply supplying random sequences of inputs to ESCORT because the system will simply give random advice on situations which, in most cases, will not test the validity of the knowledge bases.

The procedure was to take tape recordings from a gateway computer of the actual process history of the Grangemouth plant over a period of time, together with information from the plant operators on the actions they took when particular situations arose. Each tape carried a complete record of all the information made available to the operators during the period and each could be run with ESCORT to provide a realistic set of inputs to the system. Process engineers were then able to compare the advice generated by ESCORT with the action taken by operators in the real plant, and could study the hypothesis networks on which the advice was based.

A complete check of every conceivable situation is impossible in a system with so many inputs. The best that can be done is to re-create actual situations from the plant and to produce simulation tapes in which large numbers of faults are created in quick succession to check the real-time response capability of the system.

MATURATION OF THE KNOWLEDGE BASE

It is important for the system to achieve a fair degree of reliability before it is released to real-time working in the process plant control room, otherwise it will not be treated seriously by the operators. Nevertheless, there will be a period during which the system is functioning as a 'trainee'. Operators will note its recommendations and either accept or reject them. Whenever the advice is rejected, ESCORT stores a complete record of all the plant information leading up to the decision so that, later, it can be analysed in detail by the process engineer and, where necessary, the knowledge bases can be modified. Besides the plant history information stored by ESCORT, the plant process computer also maintains an historical record which can be printed out in graphical form for use by the engineer.

The original intention was that ESCORT would simply advise the operator, who would then take appropriate action in controlling the plant. As confidence has grown, however, ESCORT has been given the additional ability to carry out its own recommendations in controlling the plant. There are four levels at which the system can operate:

- 'Propose' is the basic level at which ESCORT simply reports a situation and suggests a course of action.
- 'Permit' allows the operator to authorise the proposed action, by pressing a key on the keyboard, and ESCORT carries out the action.
- 'Inhibit' gives the system the power to carry out its recommendation after a predetermined period, unless prevented by the operator.
- 'Auto' is the final level, when the system carries out its recommendation automatically and simply puts a message on the screen telling the operator what it has done.

Obviously one would only go to the final stage with relatively minor tasks and, then, only after lengthy experience has proved the reliability of the system. However, this facility will allow the operators to concentrate their attentions on the more critical areas of the process plant.

COSTS AND BENEFITS

Quantifying the benefits and costs of a large system such as ESCORT is not easy and, perhaps, the best recommendation is that BP expects to go ahead with further applications of this type. Grangemouth was the first full-scale application, in which both PA and BP were breaking new ground. Hence, from a cost point of view, it is better to think in terms of future applications in which new knowledge bases will be created on the foundation of software which is, to a large extent, already written and tested – though large real-time process plant expert systems will always have a bespoke element.

On the cost side, one has to think in terms of three phases for a large project:

- Specification.
- Implementation.
- Maturation.

Taking all three phases together, a typical large ESCORT system is likely to cost the user something in the region of £600,000 (in 1988 terms) with implementation over a period of about 12-15 months. Of this total about £170,000 would be for the computer hardware. An important part of the remaining cost would be in the time, required of process engineers, to build the specific knowledge bases. This will vary according to the size and complexity of the plant.

Building the knowledge base takes place in two stages. Primary knowledge – coming from existing records such as P&I diagrams, schedules and basic plant knowledge – can be entered during the creation of the expert system. Secondary knowledge is the detailed plant knowledge, often in the form of rules of thumb, which has to be built up, on site, with ESCORT connected to the process control system. For large applications, in the oil and gas industry, primary knowledge engineering is likely to occupy at least 25 man-weeks and secondary knowledge engineering will be spread over the life of the system.

Quantifiable benefits from a system of this type concern improved plant efficiency and reliability and may come from a number of sources. The chief sources will probably be:

- Crisis avoidance.
- Equipment problem warnings.
- Handling of complex process interactions.
- Past event analysis.

Crisis avoidance savings are not easy to estimate because major shut-downs caused by crises, it is hoped, do not happen often. However, the oil and gas industry also experiences many minor disruptions which could be avoided if operators were able to take appropriate action in good time – the sort of situation where ESCORT can provide timely advice. To obtain some measure of the potential saving, PA carried out an analysis of the records from one plant and found that minor shut-downs, which could have been avoided with advice generated by ESCORT, had cost hundreds of thousands of pounds in the course of a year.

Substantial costs come from failures and apparent failures of equipment such as transmitters, analysers and sampling systems. Quite a significant part of the total cost is incurred when equipment has not failed although operators think that it has. In one investigation, of a large plant in the oil and gas industry, operators reported instrumentation problems at an average rate of 12 per day. It was found that 25% of these were common faults, 15% were installation faults and 15% were not faults at all although expense had been incurred because engineers were sent to investigate the equipment. An ESCORT installation would have avoided the non-fault reports altogether and could have identified other genuine faults which had escaped operators' attentions. A cost analysis indicated that savings from these causes alone would amount to hundreds of thousands of pounds.

In plants where there are complex interactions between processes it can be difficult for operators to maintain an optimum regime, especially where events happen either too quickly or too slowly to be obvious to the operator. An ESCORT installation can detect and report on such interactions and may even be able to close the feedback loop and exercise automatic control. How much can be saved in such a situation depends on how much is currently being lost by operating at less than the optimum level.

Analysis of past events can lead to substantial gains in the future efficiency of a plant. However, engineers are frequently inhibited from carrying out thorough analyses because of the difficulty and frustration of working through very lengthy print-outs of plant history. ESCORT maintains a history file and is structured to analyse problems from past events. It is designed for ease of use by the engineer who can build the lessons from past experience into the knowledge base as part of the maturation process of the expert system. The quantifiable benefit from this will depend on how frequently such analyses are being carried out and acted upon.

Taken together, the quantifiable benefits from installing an expert system for real-time process plant control will, in many cases, exceed the cost of installing such a system within a year. Yet another consideration, when comparing the ESCORT approach with some other expert system shells, is the ease and speed with which process engineers can learn and use the procedures for building the knowledge base. Engineers' time represents a major part of the total cost of building an expert system and, if they are hampered by having to express their knowledge in something approximating to a computer language (such as Lisp), the time needed will be greatly extended compared with the ESCORT approach. In one comparison ESCORT was shown to save, in process engineers' time, the equivalent of half the cost of a complete system.

LUCAS – DEVELOPING EXPERT SYSTEMS FOR ENGINEERING AND MANUFACTURING

AEROSPACE and automotive manufacturer Lucas Industries has a number of expert systems in operation. These were created and implemented by the group's consultancy company Lucas Engineering and Systems (LE&S), which provides a service to external clients as well as consultancy to the group in:

- Business information systems.
- Business and manufacturing systems engineering.
- Manufacturing technology and engineering.

This last group covers all aspects of advanced manufacturing technology – manufacturing processes, design for manufacture and advanced machine systems – automation, robotics, vision systems and so on, software for computer integrated manufacturing and software for quality and expert systems. This last activity, having been rather more speculative and long-term than many others, has had a large proportion of its income from corporate funding, though there is an increasing amount of work commissioned by operating companies.

Interest in expert systems at Lucas began in 1984 when the director of manufacturing technology, John Parnaby, felt the company ought to be looking into expert systems as a strategic advanced manufacturing technology. One person was allocated to spend six months reviewing what was going on in the USA and in this country and to write a report on what the company should be doing during the following five years in this technology. He identified diagnostics as one of the most immediately fruitful ways of approaching expert systems. As a result of this, a second appointment was made, in 1985, and the team of two started work on a diagnostic application to run on a PC-type computer – as personal computers (PCs) were a low-risk investment.

The pair used the Micro Prolog language package, implemented on the PC, and a Prolog tool-kit called APES – mainly because there was not a great amount of choice at that time for PC implementations. The team members decided on a language rather than a shell because they felt it offered the flexibility they needed and, also, because it would help them to become familiar with the technology. APES was a fairly limited tool-kit for building rule-based systems. It had a query system for asking questions of the user and a simple explanation facility.

FAULT DIAGNOSIS

The first expert system was created as a corporate project with a group of people working with coil winding machines. These machines were very sensitive. The tension of the wire, the type of wire, the speed of coiling and other factors were all finely tuned and the machines were liable to drift. So, the machines were breaking down at least once a day. With a bank of nine such machines, it could almost be guaranteed that there would nearly always be one machine broken down at any time.

The purpose of the expert system was to improve the maintenance of the machines. Limited success was achieved in programming with APES and Prolog. The main problems were with the user interface. It was not possible to make explanations specific enough within APES, so standard graphics and text had to be added, from outside APES, using Prolog. Another problem was in interfacing to other packages. It was important that the system should be able to interface to an existing diagnostic system, which was reporting shop-floor problems to a planned maintenance system, but the limitations of the version of Prolog used in that system gave problems with file access.

A three-month trial of the system on the shop-floor went fairly well and gave some useful insights into the way the diagnostic system was being used. For example it was being used much more by trainees than by shop-floor manufacturing people. Investigation of this revealed that there was a gap between the sort of expertise the system was supplying and the expertise needed by engineers on the shop-floor. There were three grades of users. The most highly qualified were the works engineers. Capturing their expertise of the machines was of little use to them but it was valuable to the manufacturing craftsmen because it was of a level above what they already knew. The craftsmen's expertise was, in turn, of interest to trainees.

The expertise needed by the works engineers could not be supplied because it was held by the consulting engineers who came in from supplier companies to fix serious problems when they arose. However, the system continues to be used quite successfully as a training aid.

Following on from that application, many more diagnostic applications were generated as other people in the same factory, and from other Lucas companies, began to see the potential. As these systems were fundamentally similar, the expert systems team turned its attention to writing a diagnostic shell program which incorporated all the main features of the original diagnostic system. This, too, was written in Prolog, for application on PCs, because the team now had experience with the language as well as a number of tried routines. The finally developed package was named Maintenance And Diagnosis Industrial Assistant (MADIA).

A number of the MADIA packages have been sold to companies in the group and one has been sold outside the group. The packages have then been developed, locally, into diagnostic systems. Perhaps the most interesting implementation is on a numerically-controlled Hueller-Hille multi-spindle machine tool which breaks down occasionally and displays error messages. The messages are entered into the diagnostic system which interprets them and suggests the cause and rectification procedure to be followed. Some modern machines incorporate more detailed diagnostic and error correction procedure information but the Lucas experience suggests that knowledge-based systems could play a valuable part in built-in diagnostic systems for complex machine tools.

One helpful feature of the diagnostic system is that it keeps a statistical record of all the faults that are diagnosed and, automatically, rearranges the sequence of questions it asks the user in the light of the most likely causes of breakdown. This enables a diagnosis to be reached as quickly as possible. However, this facility makes the system an unreliable indicator of the most commonly occurring faults. As craftsmen on the shop-floor become familiar with the most frequent faults, and the methods of dealing with them, they no longer need to interrogate the diagnostic system, so its statistical procedure starts to place the emphasis on the less common causes of failure.

It is a common characteristic of knowledge-based systems that, as they impart knowledge to the users, the knowledge progressively becomes redundant – until a new user comes along who needs to start further down the learning curve.

Updating and adding new rules into the LE&S diagnostic system can be done in two ways. There is a simple method which allows the end user into a 'yes/no' question and answer routine, such as "Is the pressure 60 bar?", "Is the valve open?" and so on, leading to the remedy applied. This is a sort of electronic notebook which keeps a record of the new occurrence and provides a temporary update of the expert system until either the knowledge engineer on site, or a specialist from LE&S, can look at the file, check with the user and build the new rules in permanently. The second method involves the knowledge engineer looking at the statistics file, to find if any rules have not been fired for several weeks, and asking the operator if these are still relevant. So, there are procedures for adding new rules and for removing redundant ones. The knowledge engineer on site is not a specialist in knowledge-based systems but a domain expert who has been on a training course at LE&S and has acquired a sufficient understanding of the diagnostic software to be able to update it. In practice the local expert becomes so well acquainted with the system as to be more skilled in updating it than the software specialists from the consulting company.

Typically, a diagnostic system will deal with between 200 and 400 faults. There have been no problems over speed of response, partly because the statistical system continually updates the order in which rules are invoked and, also, because the rules are ordered in hierarchies.

There is no indication, as yet, that user companies have made any formal attempts to cost justify their expert system implementations, according to LE&S. The benefits from expert systems can be considerable but are in areas which are not easily measured financially, except perhaps in the case of diagnostic systems. There is a widespread feeling, though, that knowledge is becoming increasingly important and valuable and that knowledge-based technology, which archives and maintains that knowledge, must be beneficial.

ADHESIVE SELECTION

A system developed by LE&S for a specific application was STICK, an expert system to aid in the selection of adhesives. One of the services provided by LE&S for group companies is a consultancy on adhesive bonding and joint design and the company has a specialist who works on this subject on a part-time basis. It was she who asked for an expert system which could serve four purposes:

- It would act as a prompt on the questions to be asked in selecting an adhesive for a particular set of environmental and manufacturing conditions.
- It could be made available to design offices to help them in making routine decisions on adhesive selection.
- It could encapsulate the company's growing experience with adhesives and be a permanent repository which would not be lost if experts left or moved to other work.
- The system would also provide an up-to-date database covering most modern materials and adhesives.

The system was developed in 1987 and covers more than 40 different adhesives. It features an optimal rule-search strategy, a set of adhesive data sheets and a 'what if' facility. It was written in Prolog and runs on IBM PCs or compatibles with at least 512k of memory. The user interface incorporates 'pop-up' menus, split-screen dialogues and English-like rule formats. It is designed so that the experts themselves can maintain many aspects of the system.

There are three stages in the selection process. First the user is asked to state the two materials to be joined. The database is then searched to find any adhesives suitable for applying to both materials. In the second stage the rule base is used in an attempt to remove adhesives from this short list on the basis of design, processing and environmental requirements such as temperature and humidity. Stage three generates a final report which lists the possible adhesives for the task and gives each an index of suitability, grading them as 'very suitable' or 'partially suited'. The report also displays the responses which the user gave to the system and the rules which were successful in deleting adhesives from the original list.

The 'what if' facility allows the user to change answers and rerun the dialogue with the altered data. This can be used to relax or tighten constraints on the design in order to work towards an optimal result. Reruns like this may produce some supplementary questions from the system, as it will not ask a question during a dialogue if the answer will have no effect on the short list of adhesives.

During the question and answer session, the expert system will ask questions about the particular application in order to assess the adhesives best suited to the operating conditions of the joint. It presents the user with 'pop-up' menus which appear as small boxes on the screen indicating the options available for the user's answer. The answer may also involve a numerical input.

Also, during this session the user can interrogate the system in two ways. Entering 'explain' calls on the rule base to display any additional text or diagrams which it may have for elaborating its question. If the user types 'rule', the system displays the rule in its knowledge base which is currently being evaluated.

The final report from the system, Fig. 1, lists all those adhesives which are suitable for the application, together with their degrees of suitability. The report gives a summary of the environmental conditions, specified by the user, under which the joint is expected to operate and lists those rules which the system has used in excluding other adhesives from the short list. This list can be particularly useful in association with the 'what if' facility because it allows the user to see the effects of changing constraints – for example, if the constraints are made more stringent, it shows which additional rules are invoked. All of this information can be printed out as hard copy and the information can be included in the design process to document the decisions being made.

For the past two years the system has been out for evaluation with some group companies and the LE&S expert has been testing it against her actual decisions. In the light of this experience, the system was being updated at the end of 1989 and Lucas was considering marketing it as a product.

TAGUCHI SYSTEM

Perhaps the most important expert system developed so far by LE&S has been one to assist in the application of the Taguchi method for design of experiments. Genichi Taguchi is a Japanese statistician whose ideas on quality costs are having a considerable international impact on industry in two directions. One concerns his measurement of quality negatively, in terms of the loss associated with every product

```
ADHESIVES                                              Glass              Metals

Epoxide 1 part heat Liquid-paste                         2                   1
Epoxide 1 part heat Tape-film                            2                   1
Epoxide 2 part cold-cured                                2                   1
Epoxide 2 part warmed                                    2                   1
Plastisol                                                2                   1
Polyurithane                                             2                   1
Acrylic Anaerobic TS cold-cure + accelerator             2                   1
Acrylic Non-anaerobic 2 part cold-cured                  2                   1
Epoxy 1 part heat Liquid-paste                           2                   1
Epoxy 2 part cold-cured                                  2                   1
Epoxy 2 part warmed                                      2                   1


ENVIRONMENTAL CONDITIONS :-

You told me that the maximum temperature under which the joint is to operate is 70 deg.C
You told me that the Gap which the adhesive is to bridge is 0.1 mm
You told me that the joint width which the adhesive is to cover is 2 mm
You told me that the load which the joint is to bear is 4.5 MN/sqm

You told me that the joint is to be permanent
You denied the joint is to be coaxial

You denied the joint is to be exposed to chemicals

You denied the joint is to endure peeling , cleavage or impact
You denied the joint is to endure rotational shear
You denied the joint is to endure distortion

You told me that the seal is to be positive

You denied the length of the cure matters

You told me that a heat-cure is O.K.
You told me that a two-part is O.K.
```

Fig. 1. Final report from the Lucas STICK adhesives selection system

shipped. His other major contribution is in the development of a method for design of experiments which greatly reduces the number of experiments that must be carried out to give confidence in a new product design – and it is here that the LE&S system is proving useful.

A new design will have a number of features which can influence its overall quality, and variations in some of these features will be more critical than variations in others. Also, some factors can be controlled while others – known as 'noise factors' – have a variability which is inherent in, for example, the way that components are made, and these cannot be controlled.

Taguchi focuses attention on the relationship between controllable and noise factors with the aim of achieving high quality for the least cost resulting from factors like tight tolerancing. Setting up a series of experiments in which every controllable factor is varied independently would be impossibly long and expensive but Taguchi offers a way of deciding on an 'orthogonal array' of tests which will allow a quite small number of experiments to give a dependable result. Choosing the appropriate one out of a number of standard test arrays is a quite complex and time-consuming technical decision and the

Lucas expert system was developed to tackle this task.

The funding, in this case, came from five operating companies in the Lucas group which were introducing Taguchi methods on a large scale but which were having difficulties in training designers rapidly enough to a sufficiently high level of expertise. Together they agreed on a proposal to LE&S that a Taguchi program should be developed and they were prepared to support the work with a contribution of £25,000.

Development was helped by the fact that LE&S had four Taguchi experts who were advisers to the group and who were able to work with the knowledge engineers in developing the expert system. Discussion soon revealed that the Taguchi method was extremely suitable for the expert system approach, involving, as it did, a number of rules of thumb and a certain amount of fuzzy logic. In view of the fact that the four Taguchi experts had a target of training 450 designers in 8 months, followed by consultancy and back-up, it was decided that an expert system which could do even a small proportion of the designer's work would give a very worthwhile saving in time.

A proposal was put to the Taguchi Steering Group, consisting of representatives from the five different Lucas companies, and it was agreed to fund the initial stage of the development work. There was to be a phased introduction of the system, in which the first two phases would be useful in their own right, leading up to a full implementation in the final phase.

The earlier stages of the Taguchi design technique were selected, as shown in Fig. 2. In essence, three stages are involved in this part of the Taguchi method:

- Selection of factors.
- Selection of interactions.
- Deciding on the appropriate array.

In the first two stages, the contribution of the expert system is a matter of decision support. The engineers know which factors they want to consider and the system simply gives on-line help and explanation, to support as they decide on the two levels at which each control factor is to be tested. In the second stage any likely interactions between different factors have to be identified and here, again, the system provides on-line guidance.

The final stage involves the automatic fitting of the data to an orthogonal array and it was this stage that required the use of several sorts of knowledge representations – an important one being

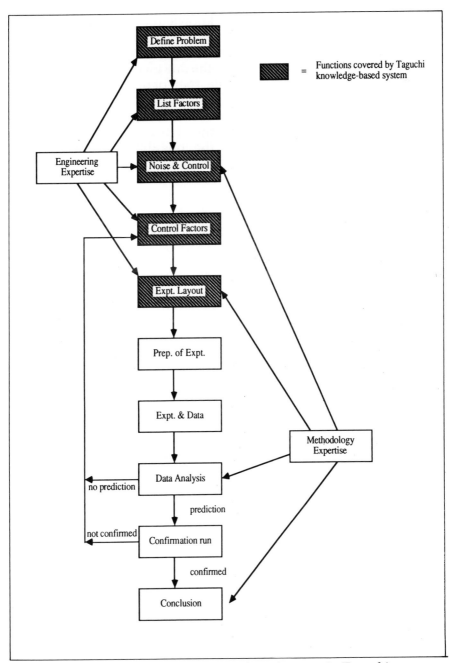

Fig. 2. Functions covered by knowledge-based system in Taguchi methodology

described as 'meta-knowledge' – 'knowledge about knowledge'. Fitting an array to the data can be a lengthy process so, rather than carrying out trial fits of arrays, an explicit rule about each array is stored and used by meta-knowledge to find the one giving optimum fit. Fig. 3 shows examples, first of a meta-rule, then of one of the array rules. These show just some of the criteria in an array rule which may be used to select candidate arrays. Some of the knowledge in the array rules has been collected from experience rather than calculated. These rules of thumb, therefore, leave open the possibility of an error of judgement in using the system, just as would be the case with human experts.

AN ARRAY IS A CANDIDATE IF
  THE DESIGN DATA HAS BEEN CALCULATED AND
  THE DESIGN DATA DOES NOT EXCEED ANY OF THE ARRAY RULE LIMITS

ARRAY RULE:
  ARRAY = L12
  MAX. NUMBER OF EACH TYPE OF PARAMETER = 11
  TWO-LEVELS
NUMBER OF COLUMNS = 11
  MAXIMUM NUMBER OF INTERACTIONS ALLOWED = 0

Fig. 3. Examples of a meta-rule and an array rule in the Taguchi knowledge base

Logic programming of the Taguchi system was done in Prolog, which was used to automate the fitting of the array, allowing the user to select the one most suited to his needs. In making this choice, the user needs to know how the fit has proceeded so it is important to have an explanation facility within the knowledge-based system. Explanations generated are aimed at several levels of methodological understanding.

The system generates a list of all the arrays which are possible for the user's design (see Fig. 4). It selects one which will produce the most statistically reliable results and offers that as its proposal. It does not take into account, for example, that the most statistically reliable array may not be the smallest array possible. If the design is one for which tests are very expensive, the user may prefer to keep the number of tests to a minimum. On the other hand, using the smallest array may lead to uncertainty about the final results so there is an element of trade-off in the user's decision.

The system also has the ability to generate 'canned text' associated

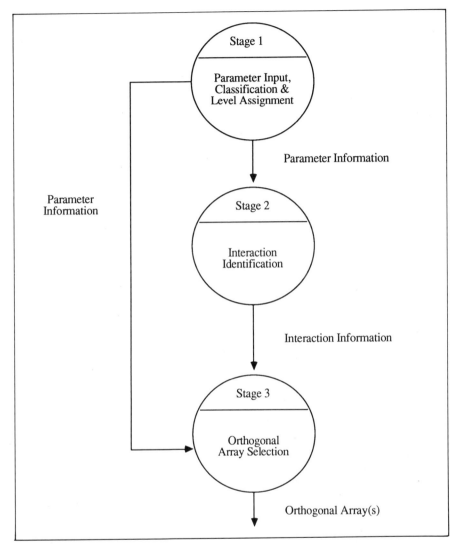

Fig. 4. Taguchi approach to parameter design

with the work it does in fitting an array. The text can be used to make
general suggestions for changes to the initial experimental design and,
for arrays which have been successfully fitted, it may make comments
suggesting design changes which could improve the reliability of the
results or increase the number of parameters which the user may wish
to consider.

At another level, users who understand the statistics of the Taguchi method can obtain much more detailed information on why particular arrays were accepted or rejected and an account of the precise data manipulations undertaken by the system. This facility makes the system of interest even to the most expert of users.

The system was developed by the team of two knowledge engineers and the Taguchi experts, using a mixture of informal conversations, structured interviews, walk-throughs of previously documented case studies – especially where problems had arisen – and the teaching experience which the four experts had already obtained. The system was developed in modules and each module was demonstrated to the experts and refined as the project proceeded. The only changes made, after this initial prototyping, were to the on-line help system.

Development of the system took about a year, to completion of the prototype version. The prototype went for formal user trials at each of the sites involved in the project where it was used both by experienced Taguchi users and by people who knew nothing about the Taguchi method. After three months of trials, a full version of the system was issued and is now in widespread use in the Lucas group. Users in the operating companies reckon that it is reducing the time needed to design experiments, by 50% for smaller designs and by up to 80% for larger ones.

DESIGN FOR ASSEMBLY

A joint project between LE&S and Dr Ken Swift, of the University of Hull, is an expert system to assist in design for assembly (DFA). The knowledge base for this was created by Dr Swift, on the basis of extensive work he had been doing on the subject, and LE&S developed a user interface to make the system accessible to designers who had not been through the three-day training session normally associated with this technique. The software has been written as a rule-based expert system, in Prolog, and one useful consequence of this is that the question and answer session, between the designer and the expert system, follows different routes according to the answers that have been given. Thus, there are no superfluous questions, the user does not have to search for the parts of the procedure appropriate to the particular design and the session is kept as short as possible.

The computer-based procedure is most effectively employed after the initial product design specification has been prepared, following the steps shown in the flow diagram of Fig. 5. "The product specification is absolutely essential", declares Graham Hird, the

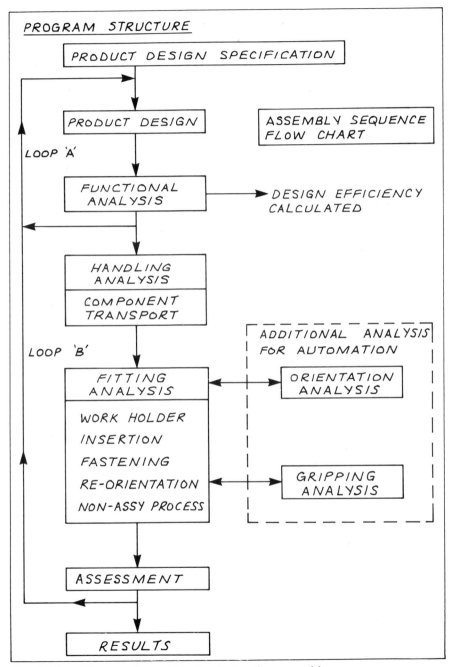

Fig. 5. Flow diagram for use by the design for assembly program

senior engineer with overall responsibility for the system. "Too many products are designed without starting from a really good specification covering not only the functional requirements but also things like customer needs, legal requirements, manufacturing constraints and so on."

From the product specification, a first attempt is made at a design, together with an outline flow chart showing all the parts in the assembly and the expected sequence in which they will be assembled. The design may be no more than a simple sketch showing the functioning of the assembly and the parts from which it is built. The flow chart is generated in a standard format, like that shown in Fig. 6, but at this stage none of the figures are entered.

At this point, the first stage of the DFA software is invoked, dealing with a functional analysis of the assembly. This may well lead to a reassessment of the product design and a new functional analysis before proceeding to the other stages of the DFA software – the handling analysis and the fitting analysis, followed by an overall assessment. If automatic assembly is envisaged as a possibility, an extension of the fitting analysis is invoked with a number of additional questions.

To give some indication of the way in which the system is used, Fig. 7 shows typical questions and messages that arise during a handling analysis which is carried out for each part in turn. When the part number is keyed in, the system recalls the information already entered. First the program asks which of a list of ranges of weights for the part is appropriate, whether its general shape is rotational and what its approximate diameter and length are – or its dimensions if it is a non-rotational part. All of these questions are relevant in deciding whether a part is suitable for bulk delivery and orientation by, for example, a bowl feeder or whether its orientation should be maintained from the previous manufacturing operation.

Next, the program proceeds to a series of questions about classical problems that arise in transporting parts – "Does it tangle?", "Is it abrasive?", "Does it nest?", "Does it adhere?" and so on. A request for more information on tangling produces the question, "Does it have open features or projections which cause tangling in bulk, or require some manipulation to separate them out – for example circlips, wire and pressed components, open-ended coiled springs?". A "Yes" answer to the tangling question produces further questions like "Is force required to separate the parts?" and "Does separation require reorientation?"

At the end of the handling analysis of each part, the system assigns

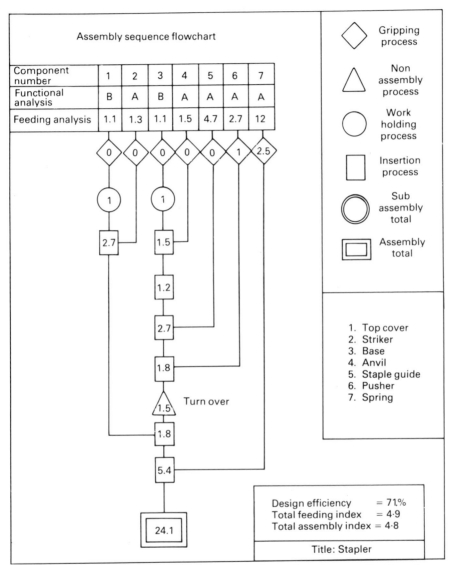

Assembly sequence flowchart

Component number	1	2	3	4	5	6	7
Functional analysis	B	A	B	A	A	A	A
Feeding analysis	1.1	1.3	1.1	1.5	4.7	2.7	12

◇ Gripping process

△ Non assembly process

○ Work holding process

□ Insertion process

◎ Sub assembly total

▭ Assembly total

1. Top cover
2. Striker
3. Base
4. Anvil
5. Staple guide
6. Pusher
7. Spring

Turn over

Design efficiency   = 71%
Total feeding index   = 4·9
Total assembly index = 4·8

Title: Stapler

Fig. 6. Completed flow chart for a typical product, showing results of analyses

it a handling index together with a breakdown of the items which have gone to make up the total figure and, possibly, a recommendation, such as "Consider retained orientation" for a heavy or awkward part. The value is entered in the appropriate 'feeding analysis' box in the flow chart and, when all parts have been analysed in this way, the computer calculates a total feeding index which is the sum of all the

---

Handling Analysis of 4 Bolt Gearbox

Question: Does the part tangle?
Explanation:
Does the part have open features or projections which cause tangling when in bulk, and will require some manipulation to separate out?
E.g. Circlips, some wire and pressed components, coil springs where the wire diameter is less than the free helix spacing.

Press Enter to continue.

Handling analysis questions determining ease of handling

Handling Analysis of 4 Bolt Gearbox

Question	Response
Can the part be supplied 'off the roll'?	no
Can the part be supplied in stick or strip form?	no
Is the part damageable?	no
Is the part deformable?	no
Does the part adhere?	no
Does the part tangle?	yes
Dose the part nest?	no
Is the part too abrasive?	no

↑ = up   Enter = finished
↓ = down   Space = toggle options F3 = stop analysis

Help message explaining question on tangling

Insertion Analysis of i2 Insert Piston

Is alignment or positioning difficult?

Options

yes
no

F1 = explain
F2 = rule
F3 = stop analysis

Explanation_____

Alignment and position of the part during insertion can be made difficult if there are problems such as:
   No lead or entry chamfers on parts.
   No lead-in shank on threaded parts or pilot diameters on threaded holes.
   Closely toleranced holes and shafts that tend to snag.
   A definite orientation is required, e.g. inserting a shaft with splines.

Question and explanation in insertion analysis routine

Fig. 7. Typical messages during a handling analysis as part of the Lucas design for assembly expert system dialogue

separate handling index values, divided by the number of 'A' (essential) parts. This value is entered in the flow chart summary.

An interesting feature of the development of this system during user trials was that a two-way process was going on. Users of the system were able to comment on it to improve the user interface but, in some cases, they found they were also reassessing the way they were analysing their designs from the point of view of easy assembly. The expert system was helping to change not only the knowledge on which decisions were taken but also the theoretical basis of the decisions.

Following on from that work, LE&S is participating in an integrated design and assembly planning (IDAP) project which is part of the major seven-nation FAMOS programme under the European EUREKA programme. IDAP aims to extend design for assembly into computer-aided design (CAD), providing an expert system interface which can give immediate assistance on designs generated at the CAD terminal, with the emphasis on design for robotic assembly. Besides advising on the creation of a design which can be produced automatically, the system will help in planning the operations – determining the assembly sequence, the types of robots that will be suitable, design of grippers and so on. The system will not necessarily tell how best to assemble a job automatically but it will point out possible difficulties in assembling particular components.

LE&S expects to see many more expert systems appearing in the product design area during the next few years, both within Lucas and in industry generally.

For historical reasons, of availability and cost, LE&S started its work on expert systems using an artificial intelligence language, Prolog, and, having built up a library of routines and techniques, has continued along the same route, though there have been some excursions into simple frame-based systems using inheritance algorithms.

If the company were starting from scratch now, it would probably start with a tool-kit with advanced frame-based representation, though the company is very conscious of the fact that large tool-kits, like KEE, require a lot of learning and even very experienced people generally use only a small proportion of the available facilities. The company still does not see a place for proprietary shells in the type of work being handled by LE&S, reckoning that shells still lack the versatility needed for the present range of work, though some of them are improving in scope.

Even for a consultancy serving a large group like Lucas, the cost of buying and developing skill in using a major tool-kit makes it a debatable proposition, especially as there is little to help the prospective buyer in deciding on the most appropriate software. There needs to be an application in view which has very strong cost justification.

JOHN CRANE SEALS –
SUPPORT FOR TECHNICAL SALES

JOHN Crane International, a member of the TI Group plc, is the world's largest manufacturer of mechanical seals, for equipment such as pumps and compressors, with a world-wide network of operating companies.

The number of different seals made by John Crane is large – there are over 150 seal types. Nearly 400 different materials are used in their manufacture, to allow them to operate in the widely differing environments presented by the thousands of different fluids – many of them highly corrosive or abrasive – which have to be pumped. Also, of course, the seals have to be made in a great variety of metric and imperial sizes. A typical seal is shown in Fig. 1.

Selecting the right seal for a particular application is a responsible and technically demanding task because many factors have to be taken into account – the designs of the pump, the stuffing box in which the seal operates and the seat against which it moves, the fluid being pumped and its temperature, pressure, speed, viscosity and so on. Until recently this has been done by John Crane's technical sales staff,

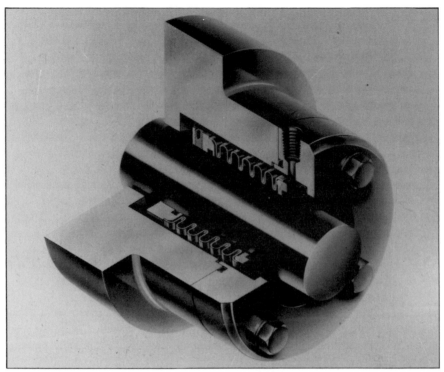

Fig. 1. A Type 515E asymmetric formed metal bellows seal from John Crane International

around the world, with the help of seal selection manuals, fluid reference books and a large number of data sheets for the individual seal types.

The drawbacks of this method of selection are obvious. The manuals are inconvenient to use, expensive and are quickly made out-of-date by the introduction of new seals and materials to meet the continually changing needs of industry to pump new types of fluids. Expert technical people have learned to find the way through the manuals quite quickly, especially when they are dealing with process plant requirements which recur frequently. However, for less experienced people, and when new or unusual situations arise, the selection task can take hours or even a day or more.

People in the company have been trying for years to find some way of alleviating these problems and the present expert system solution is the result of extended study and trials since 1984. Paul Sefton, the company's expert systems development engineer, regards the new system as an important advance but, already, he sees the scope for considerable further improvements in the future. Distribution of the system, to the company's branches around the world, began in October 1989.

Interest in the idea of using an expert system began in 1984 when the TI Group employed a person, described as an 'adhibitionist', to investigate the scope for advanced technical solutions to some of the long-term challenges facing the group. People had been thinking, for some time, about the possibility of computer assistance in seal selection but this person proposed the possibility of using expert systems – then a very new and little understood technology. The idea was taken up by John Carr, in the engineering department, who is now head of a new Engineering Systems Group with responsibilities including expert systems.

The first thoughts were to produce a computerised version of the seal selection manuals and the research department was asked to write an expert system along these lines, with technical expertise on mechanical seals supplied by the engineering department. The research people opted to use the programming language Prolog, with which they had some experience, and some of the technical engineers, including Sefton, took a course in Prolog so that they could collaborate more easily with the research project. At that time, in the UK, there was not much choice of approaches available to people starting work on expert systems.

A prototype system was completed in 1986. This was not simply an outline but a fully working system, running on an ordinary IBM PC, based on the original idea of a computerised version of the manuals. The system led the user through a series of questions in the form of a decision tree, dealing with each of the major considerations in turn. The system had a sufficiently large knowledge base to be usable in selecting a substantial variety of seals. It was used for some months internally, in the engineering office at Slough, and a number of comments were accumulated on ways in which it could be improved.

On the basis of this experience, a new version was produced and was distributed to subsidiary offices, in Europe and Singapore, as well as being used at Slough. The initial reaction was very favourable but follow-up enquiries, some months later, revealed that it was not being used. Further enquiry revealed some much deeper criticisms of the system, showing that the original aim of producing a computerised version of the manuals had been mistaken. The rigid structure of the software forced the user to follow a particular line of analysis of a problem to its final solution. To experienced engineers, this was too slow and rigid, and to less experienced people it was not easily understood.

An experienced sales engineer, approaching a particular selection task, will know from experience much of the information required to make a choice. He simply needs, for example, to see a list of those seals which are suitable for a particular fluid and temperature and can immediately select the appropriate one. It is inconvenient and frustrating to be forced to present a complete set of information, in a particular order, before the system can offer solutions, and the user may want to see what alternatives are offered when there is a small change in one of the variables.

In practice, the problem often had to be approached from a different direction. A user, wanting a replacement seal, might already have a satisfactory seat and would need a seal to match it or he might want a seat to work with an existing seal. A large chemical plant might have standardised on certain types of seals and would want to know which one, within that range, was most appropriate for a particular application.

At the same time, people began to recognise that there were other benefits to be gained if a really flexible and usable expert system could be developed.

Such a system could help to achieve *consistency* of choice, over a period of time and between different engineers. There are often many valid solutions to a particular problem but it is desirable to limit the variety as far as possible. Consistent selection helps to provide efficient manufacturing and supply management as well as helping the customer to standardise on a smaller range of seals.

A system could also be made to support the company's *marketing* strategy. It could help the company to work towards the introduction of new products and materials and to encourage older lines to move into obsolescence.

An expert system could help to capture *engineering experience* and make it more widely available. As engineers around the world encounter and resolve new problems, the experience they have gained remains with them and there are only limited ways of distributing that new knowledge around a company. A well-designed expert system should allow that experience to be fed back to the central engineering department and be incorporated in the knowledge base to be made available to everybody.

The John Crane expert system needed to be usable by people at all levels of experience so that a highly experienced engineer might refer to it briefly, to check a few facts from its large library of seals, while, at the other end of the scale, a trainee would be able to use it as a learning aid.

A fresh approach and one more fundamental than the original, was clearly needed. It would have to take much greater advantage of the capabilities of knowledge-based systems. This time, the Engineering Systems Group took on the task and, to help in faster software development, acquired a copy of the Goldworks tool-kit which is a relatively inexpensive Lisp-based programming environment.

The new system, taking account of all the criticisms and the enlarged horizon envisaged for it, was completed in prototype form by early in 1989. It was extensively tested, at Slough and in the USA, with comments being obtained from large numbers of visiting engineers. In the light of all these comments, a first, fully operational system was developed and was delivered in October 1989 with, initially, 10 copies going out to the main international offices (see Fig. 2).

After a period of experience with this system, it is intended to create a lap-top computer version of the system for use by engineers in the field. By the very nature of the product, there will never be a fixed and final version of the system and developments can be expected in the inference software as well as in the knowledge base but Sefton is confident that the main outline of the system now meets the needs of the engineers.

In its new form, the main part of the system uses just one screen display supplemented by various 'windows' giving additional infor-

Fig. 2. The John Crane seal selection system in use

mation. There are areas of the screen for entering the type of fluid, temperature, pressure, speed and viscosity, details of standards to be followed, and so on. As these values are entered, another area of the screen presents a list of all the types of seals that are acceptable for operating under the given conditions. The display can also be used in the opposite way – entering the name of a particular type of seal will produce details of the maximum operating conditions under which that seal can be used.

There are many refinements. For example, entering the name of a chemical, such as sodium, will cause a window to be displayed on the screen showing all the sodium compound chemicals for which seals are available. Units of measure can be changed instantly for each box on the screen. The temperature box, for example, can be switched between Celsius, Fahrenheit and Kelvin without affecting the other boxes. One subtle feature, though, is that, when the box for entering the diameter of the shaft carrying the seal is switched between metric and inch sizes, the list of seals also changes to reflect only those which are available in either metric or inch sizes.

John Crane International is divided into three operating areas: John Crane UK Ltd. serves Europe, the Middle East and Africa; John Crane Inc. covers all of the Americas; and John Crane Far East covers the Pacific basin and Australasia. Each of these areas has a subset of the whole range of seals which it tends to use, exclusively or in preference, and the expert system has the facility to display only those seals which are on the lists of a particular company.

There are further screen displays, giving detailed information about the seals and seats and their installation requirements, and information about liquids and seal materials.

Reflecting the need to feed back and make use of comments and advice from the field, there is a facility for the user to make any sort of comment – on a particular seal selection problem, on some inadequacy in the way the expert system functions or on any other relevant matter. The comment is stored in a computer file. Periodically, this file will be returned to Slough for analysis by Sefton. If a comment relates to the operation of the expert system he may be able to incorporate the suggestion in the next release of the software. If it is a new piece of experience on the selection of seals, he will consult with the specialist engineers at Slough and the author of the comment and, where appropriate, will incorporate the new ideas in the next release of the knowledge base.

A further valuable facility is that, when the selection of a seal has been completed, the system will print out an order form, fully documented, for sending back to headquarters and with a copy for the customer. If the local sales engineer finds that he cannot identify a suitable seal, perhaps for a new type of fluid or unique operating conditions, the computer will print out a fax message, for transmission to Slough, containing all the factual information that has been entered during the attempted selection process. The fax message is addressed to the engineer at Slough who has direct responsibility for that type of application – so ensuring it reaches him immediately for prompt attention.

The present system will run on an ordinary PC/XT-type computer, occupying about 5Mbytes of hard disk space, but the Goldworks tool-kit, under which it runs, requires a greatly extended random access memory of 5Mbytes. This is one reason why Sefton is now thinking about changing to another tool-kit. The major reason, though, is that he is now planning a further step – that of transferring the system to a mainframe computer – which Goldworks does not support.

The idea of a mainframe version of the expert system has come from a growing realisation of the wider possibilities of such a system. The mainframe version could not take the place of the portable systems used by engineers in the customers' plants but it would have the great advantage of being able to interface to John Crane's other major databases and business systems.

The main offices of John Crane around the world already have direct links to the company's mainframe computers, so the integration of the seal selection expert system is, in principle, perfectly feasible. A mainframe system would also be able to handle a larger knowledge base, incorporating graphics for seal design, installation data and so on. Updates of a mainframe system could be simpler and more frequent without the need to dispatch copies on disk to offices around the world. As is so often the case with expert systems, the scope is limited only by the imagination.

The major benefits will be realised as the system becomes firmly adopted in John Crane offices and other sites around the world. They are expected to appear in faster, more consistent and more reliable recommendations and a higher customer appreciation of John Crane's technological experience.

CLARKS SHOES – KNOWLEDGE-BASED SYSTEMS AID COMPLEX SCHEDULING

CLARKS Shoes is bringing expert systems technology to bear on the difficult decision-making involved in loading work of high variety for manual assembly. The company has adopted the approach of sponsoring one of its employees through a master's degree course which included, as a project, the modelling of a shoe production line using knowledge-based systems techniques.

Shoe manufacturing's problems of production scheduling and work loading are not, fundamentally, different from those of engineering or other industries but they are particularly difficult. For every style of shoe manufactured – of which there are many, with fashion demanding changes every year – there are a number of different sizes and, probably, different fittings and different colours. The mix of customer demand is highly variable and largely unpredictable.

To cope with the fluctuations, Clarks, which is Britain's biggest shoe manufacturer, carries a stock of about 2.5 million pairs of shoes in its automated warehouse at Street in Somerset but there is continual pressure to minimise this level because a change in fashion –

particularly nowadays in children's shoes – can easily result in redundant stock.

The most difficult stage of shoe manufacture, from the point of view of production control, is known as 'closing' which is the stitching and finishing of the upper. The work is manual, assisted by a variety of machines for stitching, eyeletting and so on. Much of it is highly skilled. To some degree it is repetitive but different styles of shoes require different treatments. Work is done in lines of about 20 operatives, working on either side of a conveyor track which takes boxes of work to and from a buffer storage area known as the 'racks', controlled by a loader who sends work to people along the line when they request it.

Work is done in 'tickets' of 12 pairs of shoes which stay together throughout their time in the factory. The name 'ticket' is used both for the bar-coded document which identifies and travels with the work and for the 12 pairs of shoes themselves. Stations on the line are equipped with machines to support all the necessary tasks and there is some duplication of equipment, giving greater flexibility. Also, the operators have acquired skills at different tasks and some have a wider range of skills than others so can be moved more readily between stations, when necessary, to balance the work-load. Each line may have, typically, six different styles of shoes in production at any time, with substantial differences in the skills and the balance of skills required between styles.

A piecework system is in operation and it is in the operatives' interest, as well as that of the company, to have a continual supply of work because they receive a lower rate of pay if they are waiting for work.

If a mistake is made on an upper – perhaps a line of stitching slightly misplaced – the entire ticket of work is sent back to the cutting room. A new piece of leather is cut, to replace the one that has been badly stitched, the stitching is unpicked, as far as necessary, and the ticket repeats its journey through the closing line as a priority job while the one defective upper is remade. The person who made the mistake does her work in her own time. The reason for keeping the ticket together is that any other procedure would further aggravate the difficult task of keeping track of, perhaps, 1,200 pairs of shoes being worked on in a closing line in the course of a day.

There are three levels at which these highly complex scheduling and loading tasks make heavy demands on the skill and experience of supervisors and, at each level, the company is looking to knowledge-based systems, together with computer-aided data collection, for assistance. At the lowest level, the line loader's ability to keep everybody on the line continually occupied, on work for which they are well qualified, is vital to the performance of the line as a whole. However, this, in turn, is dependent on the line being supplied continuously with a good mix of work appropriate to the people and equipment on the line. This second level is the responsibility of the line supervisors. At the highest level, the factory foreman, who may be responsible for three or more lines, has the task of converting a weekly order list, from the sales department, into a balanced daily requirement from the lines, taking into account things like absenteeism and the amount of scope for moving people between lines.

Before computer aids can be given to scheduling and work loading, there must be accurate and up-to-date information available on what is actually happening in the factory. There may be 8,500 or more separate pairs of shoes at some stage of completion in the closing room and these can take up to 3-4 days to progress through the shop-floor. The actual work content in the closing room takes, generally, less than two hours, which highlights the need for better control.

The knowledge-based systems project is being launched at the company's Plymouth plant – where there are two factories, each with three closing lines – because an experimental auto-routing system is already in use there as well as a full computer-aided production system (CAPS). The auto-routing system, known as Satratrack, was developed by the industry's research association, SATRA, and the idea is now being extended by Clarks.

Satratrack has already improved line efficiency by better allocation of work. Before this system was adopted, operatives were, largely, in control of the work allocated to them. When an operative wanted a new ticket of work, she or he would turn a hinged arm so that it extended across the delivery conveyor belt to stop any box being delivered down the line. This action signalled to the line loader that a new job was wanted and the loader would check, in the racks, for a ticket requiring an operation which could be carried out by that operative at that station. If there was a choice, and there was not a priority ticket waiting, the ticket with the earliest start date would be sent to the operative who returned finished work to the buffer store on the lower return conveyor.

This procedure is in use in all factories of the company and works satisfactorily, though it demands of the line loader a good knowledge of both the people and the processes on the line. Its weakness is that there is no control over the reserve of work held by individual operatives. If an operative signals a request for a new ticket while still having plenty of work in hand – perhaps wanting to ensure a steady flow of work – this may place somebody else in the situation of having no suitable work available, even though there is work waiting on the line.

The auto-routing system uses a camera to read bar codes on the baskets of work as they are returned to the buffer store, whereupon the records of jobs done on the work are updated automatically and the work reallocated to a station where the next operation can be performed.

Each operative on the line has a hand-held 'wand' bar code reader which is linked to the central CAPS computer. This is constantly recording very fine-grained information about who has done what jobs and how long it has taken, for use as the basis of the piecework payment system.

Special bar code 'wandings' indicate that an operative has no work or has produced a defective part. CAPS information is also used by supervisors to locate particular pieces of work in the factory. The combined information available on the CAPS and auto-routing systems forms the start point for simulation of production.

Preparation of the weekly schedule for the closing room is, at present, entirely a matter of skill and experience on the part of the foreman and line supervisors. Part of a foreman's weekly schedule of work for lines four, five and six is shown in Fig. 1. The work is divided into daily 'folders', here numbered from 74 to 78. A new folder of tickets is allocated to the lines each day so that the folder numbers on tickets in the line indicate how many days each ticket has been in progress through the line.

Each style of shoe has a name – Salome, Crystal, Portia, Jodie and so on – and, within each style, tickets have to be produced with different materials, sizes and so on. The overall weekly totals are determined by sales forecasts, with the mix of sizes and fittings based on statistical data. The foreman has the task of dividing this weekly demand into a daily allocation of work to each of the lines, taking into account the available labour, skills and equipment on the three lines.

The preliminary schedule of Fig. 1 is subject to modification, in the light of changing circumstances, as the week progresses. It can be seen that some lines tend to specialise on certain styles of shoes, while other styles – here Jodie and Lana II – are produced on all three lines. These are popular styles for which many operatives have been trained and whose allocation can be shifted between lines, without too much difficulty, in order to maintain a balanced flow of work. Some styles, on the other hand, can only be produced on a single line, probably

Closing plan for folders = 74 – 78				—— Tickets by folder ——					
Line	Style	Shoe No.	Tickets	74	75	76	77	78	
4	Salome	26D	41	0	0	0	0	41	0
	Crystal	35C	66	13	13	14	13	13	0
	Portia	35C	15	15	0	0	0	0	0
		45C	42	14	28	0	0	0	0
		55C	20	0	1	19	0	0	0
		75C	46	0	0	10	28	8	0
		85C	21	0	0	0	9	12	0
	Style total		144	29	29	29	37	20	0
	Jodie	05C	6	6	0	0	0	0	0
		15C	7	7	0	0	0	0	0
		35C	13	1	10	2	0	0	0
		45C	5	0	0	5	0	0	0
		85C	11	0	0	7	4	0	0
		95C	21	0	0	0	9	12	0
	Style total		63	14	10	14	13	12	0
	Ruth	35C	59	19	19	20	1	0	0
		45C	27	9	0	0	18	0	0
		75C	10	0	0	10	0	0	0
	Style total		96	28	19	30	19	0	0
	Pirouette	35C	24	0	24	0	0	0	0
	Lana II	45C	63	13	13	13	13	11	0
	Line total		497	97	108	100	95	97	0
5	Jodie	05C	9	9	0	0	0	0	0
		15C	11	11	0	0	0	0	0
		35C	19	2	15	2	0	0	0
		45C	8	0	0	8	0	0	0
		85C	17	0	0	11	6	0	0
		95C	33	0	0	0	14	19	0
	Style total		97	22	15	21	20	19	0
	Lana II	45C	62	12	12	12	12	14	0
	Minuet	05C	75	42	33	0	0	0	0
		35C	89	0	8	42	39	0	0
		95C	44	0	0	0	2	42	0
	Style total		208	42	41	42	41	42	0
	Line total		367	76	68	75	73	75	0
6	Lilly	05C	11	0	0	0	11	0	0

Fig. 1. Part of a Clarks weekly closing room plan for lines 4, 5 and 6. The full plan also gives details of shoe lasts, materials and so on

because fewer are made and not so many people have been trained to make them.

Distribution of tickets through the week also aims to maintain uniform flow and balance but it may be influenced by external factors. For instance, the foreman may have been warned that supply of a particular material may be delayed until the latter part of the week or there may be a particularly urgent need for certain styles.

Fine tuning of the schedule is done at two daily meetings of the foreman and the three line supervisors. One meeting is at the beginning of the morning, when likely problems are anticipated. The other is at lunch time, when a revised schedule for the day is worked out with work shifted between lines, where necessary, to maintain the balance. Where there is a bottle-neck at a particular operation it is sometimes possible to transfer a ticket to another line, simply for that operation, returning it for following operations.

When a total stoppage of a particular operation occurs, perhaps because of a machine breakdown, some very difficult rescheduling problems arise. There is no point in continuing work on other tickets for the same style, as this will cause further imbalance in the line for the next day or two. The choice, then, is of sending people home, finding other work for them, which does not involve the troublesome operation, or moving some people to other lines.

In factories which do not have continuous real-time reporting of the state of work on the lines, decisions about scheduling and rescheduling have to be taken entirely on the basis of rules of thumb, using very incomplete knowledge. However, even with the detailed information available at Plymouth, interpretation of it remains difficult and supervisors have to fall back on partial knowledge, leading to sub-optimal decisions.

SIMULATION MODEL

It is to this situation that David Trimm, a young software engineer in the CAD/CAM department, is applying his experience of knowledge-based systems. Trimm completed a master's degree course, in 1989, at Imperial College in London, during which he was sponsored by Clarks to produce a simulation model of a closing line.

He developed the model during a six-month secondment to the computer and software company Symbolics, at High Wycombe, and the model ran on a Symbolics workstation using that company's expert system software.

The model, developed by Trimm, is rule-based and its output is in the form of suggestions which may range over training particular operators to do additional jobs, proposing that certain operators should work a certain amount of overtime or short time or suggesting that certain people be moved to different tasks. The most important feature of the model is that it allows simulation of the highly variable and idiosyncratic performance of human operators so that a super-

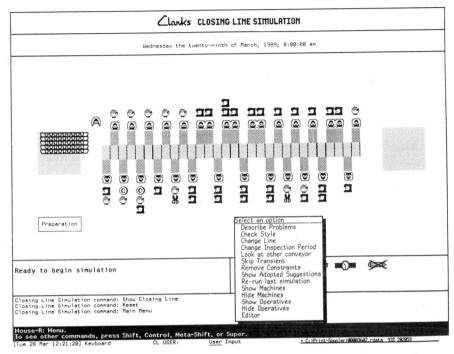

Fig. 2. Workstation screen display, from closing line simulation, shows operators and equipment at stations. At beginning of simulation, trays of tickets are all in store on the left

visor can allocate work to make best use of the available skills.

A closing line layout, taken from the workstation screen, is shown diagrammatically in Fig. 2. As already described, it consists of a number of workers who have the skills and machines necessary to carry out several of the operations on several styles of shoes. The operators are shown sitting on either side of a pair of conveyors which deliver work to and from the racks, the representation of which is shown at the left of the screen. Each 12-pair ticket is shown on the screen by a basket.

The tasks which each operator is capable of carrying out are entered in the simulation and the equipment available to each operator – which may limit the tasks the operator is able to carry out – is shown on the screen.

The tool developed by Trimm consists of four elements:

● The *simulator* which actually runs the simulation.
● The *statistics package* which is used to investigate and display the

results of runs produced by the simulator.
- The *rule base* which attempts to spot problems on the lines, automatically, and to provide suggestions about how to avoid or cater for them.
- The *editors* which allow the user to update the database – of information about machines, lines, people and styles – in a simple and visual way with as little typing as possible.

The *simulator* is an object-oriented model of the closing line environment. It is written in Flavors and Common Lisp. Flavors is an object-oriented programming language which has been implemented on top of the artificial intelligence language Lisp in some AI work-stations. The simulator allows the user to identify which production lines to simulate and how many of particular styles are to be made on those lines. Statistics can be collected as often as required during a run of the simulation and can be analysed later. There is no limit to the number of lines and styles that may be run simultaneously, though the simulator runs more slowly as more lines are introduced. Descriptions of the current status of any object in the simulation can be obtained, at any time, by stopping the simulation. Also, some objects may be altered – for instance, a supervisor may want to change the performance rating of a worker.

Nearly all user interaction at the workstation is done using a mouse and screen menus in order to reduce the amount of typing that has to be done by people unfamiliar with keyboards and computers. Animated output is also available.

The simulation distributes work to operators, taking into account their skills and the equipment available to them, allowing times for operations in relation to the capabilities of the operators. By clicking the mouse on an 'operator' symbol on the screen, the user can see a box displaying the job the operator is doing, what other work is in hand, the operator's performance rating, the expected time of completion of the current job and so on.

The *statistics package* allows simulation results to be examined by means of bar charts or pie charts. The user can see detailed breakdowns of non-productive time, how much work, at what stages of manufacture, was on the line when the statistics were collected and how the amount of work changed over the period simulated. Fig. 3 shows an example giving the numbers of tickets of work, at each stage of the closing process, held in a particular rack at the end of a simulation run. Short textual reports can also be generated, giving summaries of non-productive percentages, production rates, time

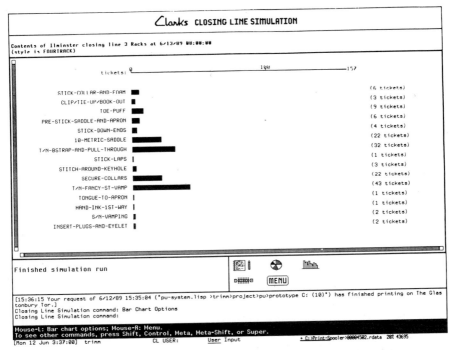

Fig. 3. Screen display of tickets in progress at the end of a simulation run

worked, least used workers, machine breakdowns and so on.

The *rule base* that has been incorporated into the simulation tool has two purposes:

● To automate analysis of the collected statistics.
● To present suggestions about what to do in problem situations.

The simulation uses an expert system rule base because the decisions taken in loading a line are not deterministic – they are founded on rules of thumb which have been worked out by supervisors over a lengthy period of experience and some supervisors are more skilled at it than others. Trimm developed the rule base through extended interviews with supervisors in Clarks factories.

To implement the rule base, Trimm used a new expert system tool-kit named Joshua. It provides a powerful extension to the Lisp language and integrates logic programming, rule-based program-ming, object-oriented methods, symbolic computation and conven-tional languages. In this particular application, it was particularly suitable because it can easily be integrated into existing code, without complex interactions or interfaces, and it is 'user tunable' – in other words, the performance of the prototype expert system can be further improved after it has been developed to a working state.

Trimm now intends to build his expert system aids to supervision, on top of a refined version of his simulation tool. At the top level he proposes to formalise the rules used by the foreman in creating his weekly schedule, to generate a schedule automatically. It will then be possible to carry out a simulated production run on each line, using the scheduled loading data, to reveal potential bottle-necks and other difficulties on the line. If appropriate, the foreman may then modify the original schedule and, at least, he will have been alerted to possible difficulties ahead.

At the line supervision level, simulation will again provide a means of checking on the consequences of emergencies on the line and of measures taken to counter them. By using the model to check their decisions, supervisors will be able to make better decisions and will be able to justify confidence in their actions.

An early goal for Trimm will be to develop tools capable of showing the consequences of interactions between lines. It is already possible to simulate several lines simultaneously but this does not include factors like transferring work between lines.

At the minute-by-minute line loading level, still greater efficiency in the allocation of work to line operatives will be achieved by combining the knowledge-based rules and real-time simulation with the auto-routing system and making use of the large volume of data in the CAPS system. Real-time reporting is obviously necessary at this level but it is also necessary if realistic simulated projections of future performance are to be made in the higher level systems.

Work has just been completed, early in 1990 on the top level weekly scheduling and simulation system and Trimm now has it running in prototype form at Plymouth.

IBM – NAVIGATING THROUGH COMPLEX DIAGNOSTICS

SIMPLE expert systems to assist diagnostic tasks are becoming quite common. They can be built relatively easily, using proprietary shells, and can often pay their way handsomely.

What IBM has achieved with the Navigator system, at the company's Greenock plant in Scotland, is of a quite different order of complexity and capability. Having been tested and implemented at Greenock, it is now being made available to other IBM plants around the world and is expected to result in significant savings in the cost of debugging printed circuit cards.

The problem addressed by Navigator is a very important one. Greenock is one of three centres in the world manufacturing IBM's new PS/2 range of personal computers and the work includes making and populating printed circuit cards for the various computers in the range. In the company's experience, the design life of a card, before it is modified or replaced by a new design, may be as short as six months – such is the rate at which the technology is developing. When a new card is introduced to manufacturing, automatic test equipment (ATE) for it, is installed in the shop at the same time, the equipment having been designed by the test engineers on the basis of the card design and their experiences of previous cards. Assembling and testing the cards is a multi-stage process and, at the end of the line, the cards are given a final box test in a customer-like environment.

During the initial days and weeks of manufacture of a new design there is a proportion of cards which fails a test at some stage of manufacture but for which the ATE is not able to supply a reason for the failure. The inability to identify the cause of failure may arise from a variety of causes. On some cards, for example, there are very fine timing constraints which the ATE cannot detect. In some cases there are problems which have simply not been foreseen in designing the test equipment.

Cards which fail for unidentified reasons have to go to manual test and it can take up to four hours of a skilled test technician's time to identify the cause of trouble in a new and unknown card. With growing experience in manufacture and testing, fewer cards fail under test, the ATE is better able to identify causes when they do fail and technicians become quicker at finding the cause when it escapes the ATE. However, even at the end of six months, some cards may have to go to manual test – which can occupy as much as an hour of a technician's time – and, after six months, there is every likelihood of a design change which will start the whole process again.

Clearly, the potential savings from faster debugging of cards are enormous and IBM engineers have been searching, for some time, to find a suitable method, looking at a variety of different approaches. The leader of the project team which developed Navigator is Bill Wright, technology performance test engineering manager, and he started with a rule-based expert system approach, using an internal IBM shell product called K-Net. The team very quickly found, though, that it was impossible to build a system on a conventional rule-based approach because the experts – the test technicians – were themselves learning. They did not know how to debug a new card – they had to find out by doing it – and by the time they had learned some rules, the product was obsolescent.

So the rule-based approach had to be abandoned but the team members had learned some useful things about the task facing them. One was the realisation that they were trying to capture knowledge from people who had a certain amount of knowledge but not enough to add up to a complete diagnostic system – so the result would be unreliable. The other major discovery was that the technicians had different styles and approaches to the job. These were so distinctive that, in one case, after interviewing Joe and putting his rules into a diagnostic chain, the team then showed the rules to Jim, who immediately said "That's the way Joe does the job. I have a better way of doing it." The team found that any rules they could assemble were rejected by the more experienced technicians, who took pride in their own methods. A the same time, these rules were insufficient to be of much help to less experienced technicians.

A fresh start was made by interviewing all the test technicians and asking them, "If you were given a knowledge-based workstation to help you do your job, what would you want it to do?" The technicians were not told what a knowledge-based workstation was – that was left to their imaginations. They came back with a large number of ideas, of which the most important related to the question of relevance. The technicians wanted access to everything that was relevant to the area they were working in. If a card had failed a particular test, they wanted to know everything relevant to that test. If they knew that there was a failure somewhere in a particular subsystem of the card, they wanted to know everything that was physically relevant to that subsystem. They also needed guidance on the steps to be taken following discovery of an error in a particular area.

Next, the project team went to see design engineers and asked if they could provide the information sought by the test technicians. The design engineers agreed that it was available, although it was distributed among a number of people.

At each stage in developing the system, the results of the team's prototype work were taken back to the two classes of users – test technicians and engineers – and they were asked if it was what they wanted, if it was usable and whether they could suggest improvements. This, highly flexible response to the users' requests necessitated the ability to build and modify prototype systems very quickly. It was also important to have a good basic representation of the physical and functional design of the card which could be accessed and used in a flexible way by the user.

These considerations pointed to the use of the KEE programming environment, which proved valuable in maintaining the momentum of the project. Users' ideas could be prototyped and presented to them in a realistic form while their ideas were still fresh in their memories. The development work has been carried out using KEE on IBM 6150 workstations but the operational versions, in future, will be delivered on PS/2 machines with KEE run-time systems.

TYPES OF KNOWLEDGE

Several different types of knowledge are used during debugging:

- *Product knowledge*. This is knowledge about the design of the product – where the components are on the card, the physical interconnections between them and so on. It also includes what the design engineers and test engineers know about the card – how it works, how its different subsystems interact and how the tests interact with the subsystems. All of this is knowledge held by design and test engineers.
- *Electronics knowledge*. This is general knowledge about electronics – the functions of different types of components, such as resistors and capacitors. It is knowledge held by both engineers and technicians.
- *Specific debug knowledge*. This consists of the tricks and techniques which test technicians learn by doing the job. Some of the knowledge they keep to themselves, some they share within the group. It is not the sort of knowledge gained by engineers.
- *Common sense*. As with most tasks, some common sense is involved and is used even by the less skilled operators who do not have specific debug experience.
- *Product debug knowledge*. When a product is first introduced, nobody knows exactly how it is going to behave on the manufacturing line or what defects are going to appear. The original rule-based approach failed because this type of knowledge does not fully accumulate until the product reaches maturity – by which time it is going out of production.

What the test technicians were asking for was access to the relevant product knowledge which could help their diagnoses. So the project team shifted its effort from trying to capture product debug knowledge to trying to get product knowledge from engineers to technicians as a first step in improving productivity of test technicians on new cards. Then, as experience accumulated, it might be possible to capture the technicians' debug knowledge and migrate that down to the less skilled operators.

PRODUCT KNOWLEDGE

The product knowledge starts with the design engineers, who

design the products, and the test engineers, who design the tests for those products. The product design is held in the computer-aided design (CAD) system which holds all the 'hard' information about the product. At the same time, a lot of the engineers' knowledge about the product goes into documentation and may also be held on computer. In principle, all this information can be transferred into a workstation for use by test technicians, though there would be a lot of work involved in capturing CAD data for use at the workstations and in presenting it in an easily used form.

It was also necessary to find some way of relating the large numbers of documents to the particular components, functions, tests and so on to which they referred and this has been done by a type of hypertext system, making use of a complex tree of relationships.

In addition, there is 'soft' knowledge, held by engineers, which may be useful to technicians in debugging a card. If, for example, a card fails a particular test, a technician needs to know as much as possible about that test. If the technician knows that the failure has occurred in a particular subsystem of a card, he needs to know everything of relevance to that particular subsystem.

The traditional expert system development procedure would be for a knowledge engineer to interview the design and test engineers and to enter their knowledge into the knowledge base. However, this method suffers from being slow and prone to error. So, to help in capturing this knowledge, the IBM development team created, from scratch, a 'knowledge editor' which allows the engineers, themselves, to record such 'soft' knowledge. The editor also allows them to import documentation and relate it to the soft knowledge. In addition, it can be used by the engineer to create new documentation.

Using this method, it takes, probably, 2-4 weeks for the design and test engineers to build up a structure of 'soft' knowledge which was formerly carried in their heads or in scattered pieces of documentation. The engineers, themselves, are very keen on using the system, which enables a large amount of design and test knowledge to be made available to the test technicians in an easily accessible form.

HOW THE SYSTEM WORKS

The systems installed on the line at Greenock (see Fig. 1) are largely mouse-driven, with an icon bar at the top of the screen indicating the different functions which a test technician may wish to call up at any time. At the bottom of the screen is a documentation bar which can be

Fig. 1. IBM test technician has access, through expert system, to design and engineering knowledge

used by the system for presenting a variety of messages. The main area of the screen is used to display graphics, such as design layouts, or documentation (see Fig. 2).

One way into the system is via an error code which has been thrown up by the automatic test equipment. Given an error code, the physical layout drawing on the screen will show shading over everything relevant to that error code – components and tracks. It is possible to show the card in greater or less detail and to 'flip' it to show the back of the card. The user can also ask to see the relevant 'nets' (IBM-speak for connections) associated with the particular error code (see Fig. 3), narrowing down, considerably, the area of search for the possible cause of trouble.

All this has been made possible by adding the designer's knowledge to the basic CAD information. However, this is just the beginning. The technician can also ask to see the logical layout of the connections on the card (see Fig. 4). Normally, this consists of 25 large sheets of paper which the technician would have to spread out on his bench. At the workstation he can display any part of the layout very quickly and can home in immediately on any particular component.

From the physical or logical layout drawings, the technician can

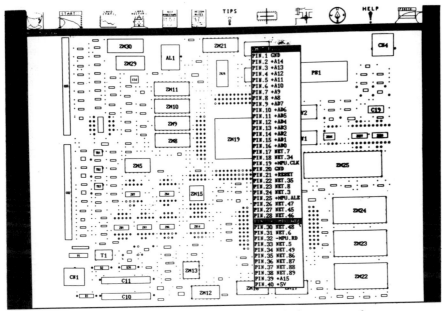

Fig. 2. Icon bar at top of screen indicates accessible functions; documentation bar at bottom displays messages

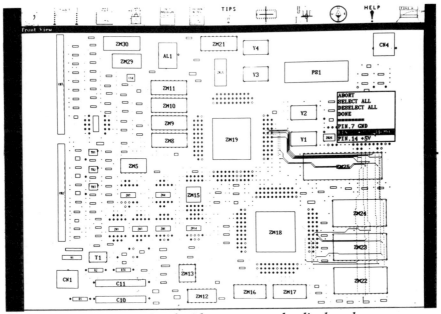

Fig. 3. Connections associated with an error can be displayed on screen

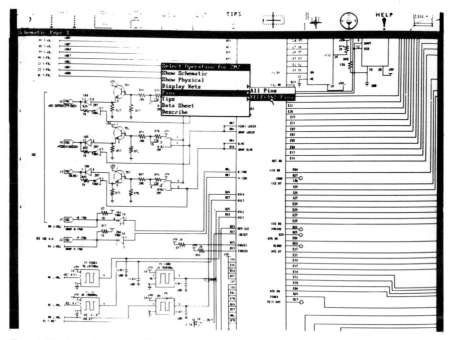

Fig. 4. Technician can call up and inspect logical layout of card – normally spread over 25 large sheets of paper

'click' his mouse on a particular component and call up information about it. He can ask for a description of it, datasheets and even scanned images of printed documentation from the published specification. He can also call up test procedures, which have been entered into the system by the test engineers, and a large amount of other information.

So that relevant information can be made readily accessible, a hypertext system is used. In every text display, key words, which point to information elsewhere in the system, are highlighted in bold type. If the user 'clicks' on one of these words, the associated document will be presented on the screen. In this way, extended chains of information about components, tests, procedures and so on can be studied.

Also accessible on-screen to the test technician is historical and statistical information – obtained by on-line access to company databases. He can inspect the manufacturing history of the card being tested, to see if it has failed earlier tests, in what respects, and what rectifications have been made on it. He can ask for statistical information on similar test failures in the past, so that he can see if there is a particular pattern of failures of which the present one is an example.

Finally, the technician can add his own remarks to be stored in the knowledge base for future reference. These 'tips' (see Fig. 5) are the only way in which the technician can add to or alter the knowledge base but they should, over the months, add a valuable fund of practical experience to the product knowledge which has been entered, in advance, by the engineers.

One of the icons on the screen is a compass card. This calls the Navigator function itself, which is a history of all the on-screen actions which have been taken by the technician in the course of carrying out a diagnosis. This is particularly valuable because of the complex chains of screen displays which may have been called up in the course of several minutes. The Navigator function allows the technician to go back, immediately, to any of his earlier screen displays. If, for example, he decides a particular line of investigation is proving fruitless, he can go back to an earlier point and pursue a different line of enquiry.

There is nothing in the system which tends to force the technician

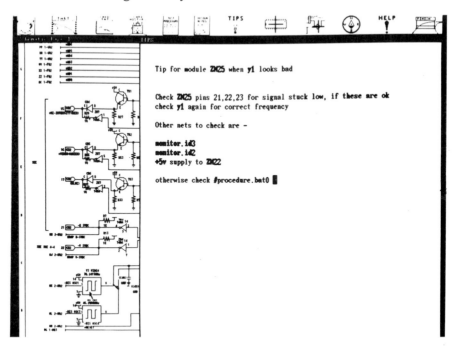

Fig. 5. Test technician can enter remarks for future reference, building experience into the knowledge base

along particular lines of investigation – it simply provides him with all the available information on any subject which he requests, leaving him to follow the direction which seems most appropriate to him. This is simply reflecting the facts of the case – at the beginning of manufacture of a new card the engineers have no more idea than the technicians of the likely causes of failures.

Although the technicians are not able to modify the knowledge base, apart from entering tips, the knowledge base is readily accessible to engineers on entering a password. This gives them access to another icon bar providing the ability to enter new error codes and to add and edit documentation.

By the spring of 1989 two systems were installed, and in regular use, on the assembly line at Greenock and final operational versions, on PS/2 machines, were being implemented as rapidly as possible. In the light of experience with the first two systems, Bill Wright is looking for several bottom-line benefits from the introduction of Navigator:

- Reduced line fall out.
- By improving the learning curve, new staff will become effective much faster.
- Improved product quality as a result of minimising repairs and achieving 'right first time'.
- Improved skill base. As the technicians use the system they are learning faster and so, are improving their skills. Knowledge-based systems are sometimes accused of depleting the skill base, by making it possible for people with less skill to do the job. In this case, technicians are gaining in knowledge as they make use of other people's knowledge.
- A 20-30% saving in scarce manpower needed for this task. This figure was estimated from careful work study and, as more diverse types of knowledge are incorporated into the system, it is expected that even greater savings will be possible.

ISSUE – AN INTELLIGENT SPREADSHEET ENVIRONMENT

SEVERAL expert systems have been prototyped by PA, some going through to full implementation, with a user/expert interface that is particularly attractive to people who are accustomed to using spreadsheets such as Lotus 1-2-3. The framework on which these are based is called ISSUE. ISSUE is not described as a shell because the environment requires some degree of tailoring to each different application.

Applications using this environment have been as diverse as arbitrage and share dealing on the one hand and renewable energy consultancy on the other. The arbitrage application was developed for an international securities firm, for use in London and New York. It is connected to a real-time price feed and a relational database and advises international equity dealers on potential arbitrage opportunities arising from inequalities between the prices of certain shares traded on the UK market and those of corresponding American Depository Receipts (ADRs) which are traded on the US market.

ARBITRAGE TRADING

The system enables different trading strategies to be modelled, tested and refined before being run live. In day-to-day operation the user can select from the library which strategy to run at a particular time. The system has four components.

Real-time feed
This is supplied by Telekurs and is interfaced to the system's MicroVax computer. Information coming from this feed consists of:

- Real-time price information on about 300 securities. This information includes bid, ask and last trade prices for various securities, mainly from the UK and US markets, though a small number of prices are received from other markets such as Paris and Amsterdam.
- Dividend information for the above securities, for example ex-date and dividend amount.

MicroVax computer
This machine carries out the following functions:

- Storage of data supplied by the real-time feed. The information received is stored in an RDB database.
- Maintenance of an ordered list of current arbitrage opportunities, with the most profitable first.
- Maintenance of 'position' information, i.e. information about numbers of particular securities currently bought and sold. This information is entered by the users.

Communications
The MicroVax communicates with the expert system computer via an RS-232 interface. Communication is initiated by the expert system machine which repeatedly:

- Requests a price message, which contains all the changes in the prices of shares and ADRs since the last message.
- Runs the price message through its model and produces a profit figure.
- Notifies the MicroVax of the profit figure.

It may then receive a message indicating that its list of current opportunities should be changed in some way.

The expert system computer
ISSUE, itself, runs on a Xerox 1186 workstation or an IBM PS/2 computer. It has been adapted so that it can run in real time or in stand-alone mode, which generally equates to operational or knowledge engineering use. In real-time mode the user views a spreadsheet on which are displayed the current best five arbitrage opportunities. The spreadsheet is updated in real time as new price information is received and modelled.

In stand-alone mode the user has full access to all the normal ISSUE facilities which include the ability to change the knowledge base and the layout of the spreadsheet on which the opportunities are displayed.

ISSUE has been designed so that its knowledge base can be created and maintained by the user. In fact, it was first developed because of a communication difficulty between an investment specialist and a knowledge engineer on a system that was being developed for Lazards, the merchant bankers. It is a slow and frustrating task for both parties when a knowledge engineer must attempt to understand the technical terminology used by the domain expert and to interpret it for the computer. ISSUE was the result of a successful attempt to eliminate this intermediate step.

There are many situations which lend themselves to the framework provided by ISSUE, not only in the world of finance. The system has been adapted to an application in the oil and gas industry, dealing with data analysis of flows in pipelines, covering such problems as discrepancies between meter readings and actual flows. ISSUE has also been used in the energy sector, where it has been applied to the evaluation of alternative scenarios in order that a given opportunity can be best exploited or the most cost-effective solution to meeting an energy requirement be found. Yet another application aids routine purchasing of raw materials in the food processing industry.

Although essentially a rule-based system, ISSUE's particular strength is the way in which the rules are structured by a network of dependencies. This structure is coupled with a highly interactive graphical interface and these two characteristics define the particular strengths of the system.

The domain expert builds the expert system at the terminal of a computer workstation which has a much larger screen than an ordinary PC and is 'bit-mapped'. This means that it can carry several windows, presenting a large amount of information as well as high-quality graphical representations. The system is created with the help of two display interfaces.

SPREADSHEET INTERFACE

One interface has the familiar spreadsheet format, with cells arranged in rows and columns. Windows can be opened in different areas of the screen to different parts of a large spreadsheet. An example, from a system giving advice on buying and selling of shares, is shown in Fig. 1.

SHARES:							Add column
	Share price	Rel. PE ratio	Manage-ment	Static fin. pos.	Short term rec.	Long term rec.	Add row Create column Create row
Company 1	220	2.74	Good	Bad	Buy	Buy	Refresh
Company 2	118	41.88	Good	Ave	Hold	Sell	Clear
Company 3	152	− 6.09	Ave	Good	Buy	Buy	
Company 4	146	3.08	Poor	Good	Sell	Sell	
Company 5	146	27.91	Poor	Bad	Sell	Sell	
Company 6	84	−50.68	Bad	Bad	Buy	Sell	
Market Ave	—	0.00	—	—	Hold	Hold	

Fig. 1. An ISSUE spreadsheet display offering recommendations on the basis of company performance

Rows in the spreadsheet represent different companies, with the bottom row showing market average values, while each column carries information on a particular characteristic of the companies. It looks like an ordinary spreadsheet and can be used like a spreadsheet in that the values in individual cells can be changed and 'what if?' investigations can be carried out by making temporary changes to see the effects. Some of the cells carry numerical information, as would be expected in an ordinary spreadsheet, but others contain textual matter which is not simply for display, as it would be in a spreadsheet, but which represents judgements relating to characteristics of the companies – such as 'management is good', 'long-term value is high' or 'short-term recommendation is to sell'.

In both ISSUE and ordinary spreadsheets some cells are linked to others by mathematical dependencies. What is unique about ISSUE is that these dependencies may also be specified by sets of rules. The rules can be presented on the screen in a form like that in Fig. 2, where the second line reads:

Good   Average   Good   Good

which translates to a rule of the type:

    if Rel.Growth.Rate is Average and Future.Growth is Good and
      Current.Market is Good then Long.Term.Prosp is Good.

Long Term Prosp.	Rel. Growth Rate	Future Growth	Current market
Average	Average	—	—
Good	Average	Good	Good
Good	High	Average	Good
Poor	Low	Bad	Poor
Bad	Low	—	Bad
Average	Low	Good	Average
Poor	Average	Average	Poor
Poor	Average	Bad	Excellent
Very good	High	Good	Average
Poor	High	Bad	Good
Average	High	Average	Poor
Good	High	Good	Good
Poor	Average	Bad	Bad
Poor	—	Poor	—
Good	High	Good	Poor
Poor	Low	Poor	Poor

Fig. 2. An ISSUE rule table in a company analysis spreadsheet

It is also possible to define cells as having dual status, so that numerical and linguistic values can be combined. For example, a numerical value may be calculated for a cell and then assessed by a linguistic rule as 'high' or 'low'.

Setting out the rules in a table, as in Fig. 2, besides allowing a very compact format, helps to give some structure to the rule table by grouping together all the rules relating to the same characteristic, for instance Long.Term.Prosp.

Another extension, which has proved useful in certain applications, is the specification of a cell's value as the result of an external database query, the parameters of which are defined by other cells' values.

BROWSER INTERFACE

Two of the difficulties in using expert system shells are understanding how the various factors relate to each other and investigating the effects of changes in the situation under consideration. The ability to deal with a range of questions that start with phrases such as 'What if . . .?' and 'Under what circumstances . . .?' is a major difference between human and computer experts. ISSUE's answer to this is to provide a 'browser' interface which shows the dependencies between the different characteristics of the companies. Fig. 3 shows such a set of relationships, for one company in the share dealing application. In the spreadsheet, the decisions mainly relate to cells in the same row across the spreadsheet, so the structure is the same for each company

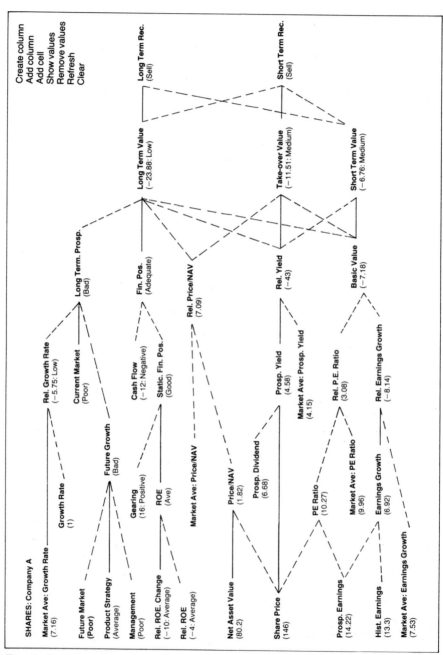

Fig. 3. Browser interface of ISSUE shows dependencies between different characteristics of companies

represented by a different row. The bottom row of the spreadsheet shows market averages, so its cells feature in the browser network for each of the companies.

With the browser, the user can see the full effects of changes at any of the nodes in the network and why the effects have been produced. It is also possible to by-pass some of the input where some conditions are not known or where an outcome is already understood. For example, in the top section of the browser, the user may know that the long-term prospects for a company are bad and can enter this directly, ignoring the inputs to the left of it.

CREATING THE SYSTEM

In creating the knowledge base, the browser interface gives the expert the ability to describe relationships involved, to test and change them and to see the consequences – all very quickly and clearly. If, for example, the system reaches a conclusion about a particular company which is seen to be wrong, the browser can be studied to identify the chain of reasoning leading to the conclusion and, if necessary, new factors can be introduced or relationships can be adjusted to improve the way in which the knowledge is handled. In particular, the use of the browser makes the broad structure of the knowledge base explicit and enables the system builder to get the 'big picture' correct before dealing with the details of individual rule sets. Other advantages which accrue include that of greatly reduced knowledge base maintenance costs – somebody with little involvement in the creation of the system can contribute effectively to its maintenance. This contrasts sharply with simple rule-based expert system shells, where both the relationship between rules and the way in which rules are used are implicit in the detail of their wording and ordering and are not easily elucidated.

Moreover, in an organisation where there are several experts making decisions based on their own experiences, these experts may wish to adapt certain elements of the knowledge base to their own assessments of the factors involved and the priorities to be assigned to them. Hence, there will be a core knowledge base which is common to all the experts, with certain aspects adjusted to suit individual preferences. ISSUE is particularly suited to aiding experts in their own work.

HELP IN TRAINING

The same facilities give ISSUE an advantage as a training aid, because the user can see not only the conclusions reached by the expert system in each case – which is all that the user of a shell is likely to see – but, also, the process of reasoning by which all such recommendations are made and the particular combination of considerations leading to the current recommendation. Use of the browser gives the user a much clearer understanding of the reasoning processes than will a simple list of steps in the decision-making process provided by most interrogation procedures.

Introduction of ISSUE has not entirely removed the need for help from a knowledge engineer because some specialist skill is needed in the initial creation of an outline network for the relationships represented in the browser. However, the input needed from the knowledge engineer is greatly reduced and is mostly at the initial stages of the project.

DIGITAL EQUIPMENT CORPORATION – CONFIGURING COMPUTER HARDWARE

DIGITAL Equipment Corporation (DEC) was one of the early pioneers of expert systems, with a highly successful system to assist in the configuration of computer hardware systems. Known as XCON, the system was introduced into the company's USA operation in 1980. In its latest version, it is in use in the company's plants throughout the world and is reckoned to be bringing a net return of more than $40 million per year.

Today, XCON is the largest of a growing number of knowledge-based tools being introduced by DEC into its information systems. Closely linked with XCON is XSEL, which supports computer sales. Another prototype system, to help in decision-making about distribution logistics, is the Logistics Modelling System (LMS). The current state of these three systems was discussed at the Expert Systems '88 conference by Arnold van de Brug and Dr Tim Barber, and the following study is based on their papers.

Knowledge-based systems are now seen by DEC as helping business decision-making, in situations where large masses of relatively low-value information are being handled. The concept of a 'knowledge lens' – which can be used to filter and focus corporate information to support the decision-making of the business professional – has been created. Seen in this way, the knowledge lens, suitably customised to the particular application, can distil the large volume of information into concise, high-value information to support consistent, timely and effective decision-making.

Barber offers a model of business activities, connected by information flows, in terms of an 'enterprise map', with three interconnected lobes – demand, supply and innovation. For example, in a manufacturing company one could summarise the information flows within these lobes as follows:

● *Demand*. The customer places orders with sales and these are passed on to order administration for processing. Details are passed to manufacturing to build the product which is then shipped, by distribution, to the customer.

● *Supply*. Manufacturing uses stocked components. Procurement reorders stock, from suppliers, which is received and handled by materials management ready for use in manufacturing.

● *Innovation*. Research look at possible future directions in the market, technology and so on. Strategic planning (marketing) decides the business direction and this strategy is distilled into new products, designed by engineering, which are fed into the business.

Information flows around these loops within the enterprise and, at all stages, business professionals are analysing the information, making decisions and feeding the results on to others. So, the concepts of 'work in progress' and the 'value chain' can be extended to 'information in progress' which is having 'value added' by processing at each stage. Within this environment, knowledge-based systems can add value to the information by consistent analysis, supporting better decision-making.

CONFIGURATION SYSTEM

Using the above descriptive framework, XCON falls within the demand lobe. It was first developed for DEC at Carnegie Mellon University, under a research project started in 1978, and was used to carry out the configuration of VAX-11 and some PDP-11 computers. It starts with a customer's order and determines what parts are needed to build it.

Customer needs vary widely in terms of scale, integration with other systems and networks, connectivity, flexibility, resources required, response times, growth and so on. To meet these needs, DEC offers a range of computing 'platforms' which can be assembled from different components. However, there are constraints on how the components can be connected and assembled as systems. XCON checks whether all the elements will work together satisfactorily, in an efficient system, and whether some substitutions, or additions would be desirable or necessary. XCON also generates print-outs showing the components chosen and why others have been replaced. It calculates and prints the cable lengths required inside the cabinet, the physical addresses of components on the computer bus and a series of diagrams, showing how the various devices and modules relate to each other physically in the cabinet and logically.

Configuring a system was formerly a task for an expert, taking about 25 minutes for each job and about 10,000 such configurations were needed per year. The work was very tedious and mistakes were frequent. Different engineers tended to configure the same sets of components in different ways, so there was a lack of consistency. As the engineers were skilled people, they tended to be promoted to other work, so there was a declining level of skill among configurers.

XCON is a rule-based system which uses its knowledge to generate a single acceptable solution to each problem. When it was first adopted it had a knowledge base of 700 rules and a database of 400 components. By 1988, the latest version was using more than 10,000 rules, of which half change every year, and a database of more than 30,000 components. From configuring a single type of computer system, XCON now embraces the configuring of 30 families of computer systems.

SALES SUPPORT

One natural extension of XCON was to provide sales staff with an aid to help customers produce computer specifications best suited to their needs – at the same time avoiding unsuitable or impossible configurations.

AMERICAN EXPRESS – AUTHORISING HIGH-VALUE PURCHASES

CHARGE card company, American Express, is using an expert system, developed by Symbolics, to help in evaluating and authorising high-value purchases by its card-holders. The aim is to maintain high member satisfaction while reducing the risk of fraud. The system helps specialist authorisers to make good decisions when they receive telephone requests for authorisation of purchases using American Express cards. About a million such requests are received every day by the company's offices around the world and something like 15% of them come within the scope of the Authorizer's Assistant expert system.

The system was developed, in collaboration with American Express, by the Symbolics Consulting Group. Symbolics is a supplier of computers and Lisp workstations and runs its own consulting service. Development began in 1986, using two Symbolics 3645 workstations running the ART tool-kit from Inference Corporation. Prototype and pilot phases took six to nine months and the production system was brought into use during 1988. This deals with 120 transactions per minute, with up to 800 rules for each transaction. If no human intervention is needed for approval, the system will supply its decision in less than 10 seconds. By the autumn of 1988 the system was handling 12,000 transactions daily.

The credit authorisation system comes into use whenever a shopkeeper, hotelier or restaurateur telephones for authorisation when a customer presents an American Express card. Most such transactions are approved automatically but any which are unusual in any way are diverted for assessment by human authorities. Assessment is made more difficult by the fact that charge cards, like American Express, do not have spending limits such as those imposed by credit cards. This increases the risk because large sums of money may be involved. It also means that different clients may use the cards in very different ways, i.e. some card-holders make frequent large purchases while others do not. The automatic system passes a query to a human authority if a proposed purchase is unusually expensive or is uncharacteristic of the particular card-holder in some other way.

The expert system comes into use when the automatic authorisation system passes a query to a human. The information passes first to the Authorizer's Assistant expert system, which applies the same rules as a human expert would to approve or reject an application. This then passes the information on to the human expert, together with its own recommendation. The system does not make the final decision in the case of a refusal.

From the card-holder's point of view, it is important to deal with referrals quickly but reliably. The average time for a referred request is 72 seconds, of which the Authorizer's Assistant takes, on average, 12 seconds. Besides passing recommendations to the human expert, the system can automatically issue approval codes if the application is accepted.

Currently, the system runs in the USA on 20 Symbolics workstations linked by a local area network at the American Express data centre in Phoenix, Arizona, where 125,000 calls are handled each day. The system serves the whole of the western hemisphere and, as it is refined and users gain experience with it, it is expected that at least 20% of referred transactions will be handled automatically by the Authorizer's Assistant. Not only will this save money, by allowing the same number of people to deal with a larger number of calls, but the system is also expected to improve the quality and consistency of decisions. It will allow relatively inexperienced people to deal reliably with queries and will assist them in gaining skill.

As many as 13 different databases of client information may be accessed by the Authorizer's Assistant in arriving at its recommendation – via the company's IBM mainframe computers. For each card-holder, a detailed 90-day history of transactions is maintained and this is supplemented by annual accumulations of some information. Certain information is also maintained throughout the lifetime of the card-holder and all this information may be called on by the Authorizer's Assistant in making an individual assessment.

Very high reliability was essential for a facility of this kind and Symbolics was able to guarantee a 99.5% up-time by supplying hardware with a redundant processor which is kept on-line all the time and can go into service within one second if a hardware failure is detected.

ACHILLES – CLUB PROJECT ON METAL CORROSION

THE Harwell Laboratory of the UK Atomic Energy Authority became interested in knowledge-based systems in the late 1970s as part of its wider interest in technology transfer. The laboratory's business today ranges very much more widely than nuclear energy and includes contract research and development for many industries, covering computer applications, materials, corrosion and many other areas of science and technology.

Both for the laboratory, itself, and for clients, efficient access to information is vital and spurred the development of a method for storing and retrieving unstructured texts of documents. This resulted in a product called STATUS which indexed every word in a document, allowing the document to be searched for any word. STATUS was originally developed for searching the text of statutes but it was ultimately marketed for a variety of applications.

One of the first rule-based expert systems produced at Harwell was written in Prolog, to help users carry out the configuration of equipment sold by the laboratory for nuclear counting. It had some similarities with the well-known XCON system developed by the Digital Equipment Corporation.

The biggest expert system project undertaken so far has been the ACHILLES club project, run in collaboration with the National Physical Laboratory, which advises users on many aspects of metal corrosion. The project began in 1986 and is due for completion in June 1990. It is described in more detail below.

Besides ACHILLES, Harwell has a number of expert system projects, either completed or in progress, some of them for individual clients, others running as club projects. A distinctive feature of the laboratory is that it employs a large number of scientists and engineers which means that, for many application areas, it is able to supply both the knowledge engineering and the domain expertise for building an expert system. The laboratory has set up a Knowledge Engineering Services Centre and Harwell's matrix management structure allows teams of knowledge engineers and experts in particular subjects to be brought together for individual projects.

An interesting recent trend has been towards greater use of proprietary expert system tools where these are appropriate. The laboratory has acquired a number of these products and is authorised to sell several of them. So, it is in a position both to advise prospective users impartially on which tool, if any, is most suitable for a particular application and also to implement systems using them.

Applications, requiring special features outside the scope of the tools, are written using the tools, in Prolog, developed by the laboratory. Lisp-based tool-kits, such as ART and KEE, have not been used and, in the present rapidly-changing market conditions, the investment in them – particularly investment in the time needed to learn such systems – is not considered to be justified.

Harwell's approach to the implementation of expert system projects is, in many ways, similar to that outlined earlier in this book but it has some distinctive features. One of these is called the 'T' method of prototyping and it is designed to counter two opposite criticisms which are regularly made of expert system prototypes. One of these criticisms comes from the specialist who looks at a prototype and says, "It doesn't tell me anything I didn't know already." The other objection comes from the person who says, "It's interesting but it doesn't cover my area of interest." The difficulty at the prototype stage is to produce something which goes into sufficient detail to demonstrate its usefulness while covering a broad enough subject area to attract all the potential users.

In the 'T' approach the aim is to demonstrate a prototype system which is broad enough to show what the scope of the final system will be – the cross bar of the 'T' – while covering one selected aspect in sufficient depth to show the competence of the final system. The objector who considers it to be superficial in his area of interest can then be shown an example of its capability in another area.

At the stage of specifying a new system, a helpful way of thinking about it, used at Harwell, is to decide where it will fit on each of the following five axes:

Advisory	<—>	Informative
Private	<—>	Public
Internal	<—>	External
Deep	<—>	Shallow
Precise	<—>	Ambiguous

The first axis indicates how far the system will take decisions and present them to the user (advisory) or provide the user with the information to take his or her own decisions (informative). The second axis concerns who owns the expertise – whether it is proprietary or public. The third axis describes whether or not the system will be used by the same organisation that wrote it – which influences questions such as maintenance of the system and design of the user interface. A 'shallow' system, on the fourth axis, would be one where experts base their decisions on a conceptual model of the process covered by the system ("I don't know why it works the way it does but this is the way to use it"), whereas a 'deep' system would incorporate knowledge about the nature of the process itself. The final axis runs between the extremes of knowledge based on physical laws and knowledge based purely on experience.

ACHILLES

The first efforts at building a system to give advice on corrosion began some years ago, before much was known about expert systems. Corrosion seemed a worthwhile topic for a computer system, being a mature subject which, though developing, is not at the frontiers of science. There is a large body of practical experience on the subject and, if it could be captured in a computer system, it would be valuable to many people who need to know what can be done about corrosion without, themselves, becoming corrosion specialists – design engineers, maintenance engineers and others.

A first step in this direction was to build a free-text database, using STATUS, covering the many technical reports on corrosion, but this was a rather limited method for accessing information, so thoughts turned to creating some sort of 'expert system' – whatever that might mean.

In the best scientific tradition, two teams set to work using quite different approaches. One team tried to build a causal model of the corrosion process, based on fundamental knowledge of thermodynamics, chemistry and so on, and to construct rules based on this knowledge. The team came to the conclusion that corrosion is too complicated a process, involving too many different factors interacting in complex ways, for a 'deep' system of this type to be feasible.

The other team set about writing down rules based on everyday knowledge about corrosion – simple statements like, "If the material is carbon steel and it is in a liquid containing oxygen then the metal will corrode." This pragmatic approach proved most successful and it is on this foundation that the ACHILLES club project developed.

Membership of ACHILLES includes a number of major international companies, including some involved in activities in the North Sea environment, chemical and petrochemical companies, and government departments like the Ministry of Defence and the Department of Energy. The project runs as a joint project between two laboratories – the National Physical Laboratory (NPL) and Harwell. NPL's National Corrosion Co-ordination Centre provides the secretariat, arranges club meetings and places and monitors contracts with outside organisations. These contracts are for the generation of resource documents on different aspects of corrosion which are to provide the raw material for the expert system modules. NPL also acts as banker to the project, as there is also funding from the Department of Trade and Industry. The Harwell Laboratory is responsible for taking the corrosion information, collected through the resource documentation contracts, building it into an integrated structure of expert system modules and databases and distributing the systems to members.

The entire field of corrosion is very large and has many aspects, so it was not considered feasible to build a single expert system to cover the entire subject. It was decided that there should be a number of separate expert system modules but with a common user interface and the ability for the user to move from one module to another, carrying across any relevant information from the previous module. The decision to subdivide the whole subject into smaller elements led to further difficult decisions about how it should be divided and how the elements should then be integrated to give the user access to them all as a single system.

The subject matter and scope of the different modules were agreed by the club members who voted on the priorities to be given to the different modules. Despite the variety of member organisations there was not much conflict of interest over what should be included in the final system and what priorities should be applied, though, inevitably, there were some differences of emphasis in what were seen to be important topics.

Having decided on the broad subject matter and scope of the different modules, check-lists were prepared and agreed, giving, in detail, the questions which the expert system should be able to answer and the problems which it should be able to solve. The results of the check-list exercise formed the basis of the formal specification for building the prototype of each system. The check-lists were also incorporated in the bids solicited from organisations which could provide the resource documentation to be used to build the expert system.

Knowledge engineering skills are particularly valuable in these early stages of framing the specification because experience of previous systems helps to ensure a suitable structure for the knowledge base and leads to the adoption of the most appropriate expert system tools.

The resource documentation, the production of which is done under contract by experienced organisations, is, in effect, a paper representation of what the expert system will cover. It may be a collection of many documents dealing with different aspects of the particular area of corrosion. Each set of resource documentation is reviewed by the club and, where necessary, modified or enlarged. Produced with the resource documentation is a glossary of relevant technical terms which might need to be explained to non-specialist users. This is then used by Harwell in the generation of a prototype system for testing and review by the users, whose comments are taken into account in building the final production system.

One further possibility is that the resource documentation is incorporated, in the final versions of the systems, as a free-text database, so that the user can refer back to the original source from which the expert system's recommendations have been derived.

The scope of this suite of expert systems and databases will be very wide when it is completed in 1990. For materials analysis, it covers questions such as:

- What should any given component be made from?
- How can it be protected?
- How will it interact with other materials?
- Will corrosion be the factor limiting its life?

It helps in the analysis of past corrosion failures – questions like:

- What was the probable cause of corrosion?
- What factors exacerbated the problem?
- What remedial methods are available?
- How can such problems be avoided in future?

It can also be used for training in practical understanding of corrosion, by providing structured knowledge in a highly interactive form which is directly responsive to the user. The modules make use of free text, graphics and tabular information to give the most effective support to the answers and recommendations which they provide.

ACHILLES is intended to provide corrosion information for people who are not corrosion experts. It is designed to tackle the 50-75% of problems which commonly recur and are well understood by corrosion scientists but are not well known by people like maintenance engineers and design engineers. The system offers the user a hierarchical series of menus which go deeper and deeper into the topic being studied. Fig. 1 shows a typical readout from the system.

The user can decide how deeply to look into a topic but the system is also interactive. It will prompt the user for particular information and will ask questions about the material he is interested in and conditions like flow rate, temperature and so on. It will, then, use this information to refine the answers it gives. It will offer numerical information, if it is available, on matters like corrosion rates and will indicate the type of corrosion that may appear – for example, in holes or in large areas. The system will indicate factors that influence the corrosion rate and what can be done to reduce the corrosion rate. It will then point the user towards more detailed information if he wishes.

There are a number of other facilities including a built-in dictionary – if the system uses a technical term or an acronym which the user does not understand, he can type a question mark with the word and the dictionary will supply a short definition. In addition, at any time, the user can see a summary of the conditions he has typed in and these can be altered in a 'what if . . .?' dialogue. So, the user can ask how conditions will change if, say, the flow rate is twice as fast.

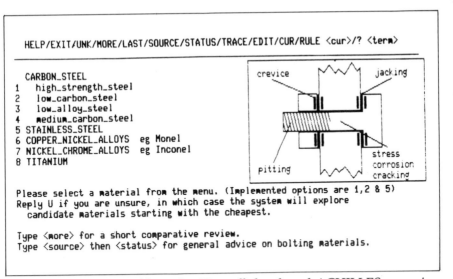

HELP/EXIT/UNK/MORE/LAST/SOURCE/STATUS/TRACE/EDIT/CUR/RULE <cur>/? <term>

CARBON_STEEL
1   high_strength_steel
2   low_carbon_steel
3   low_alloy_steel
4   medium_carbon_steel
5 STAINLESS_STEEL
6 COPPER_NICKEL_ALLOYS eg Monel
7 NICKEL_CHROME_ALLOYS eg Inconel
8 TITANIUM

Please select a material from the menu. (Implemented options are 1,2 & 5)
Reply U if you are unsure, in which case the system will explore
  candidate materials starting with the cheapest.

Type <more> for a short comparative review.
Type <source> then <status> for general advice on bolting materials.

Fig. 1. Typical readout from the Harwell-developed ACHILLES corrosion information system

There are many interacting factors affecting corrosion in any particular situation – the particular alloy and its heat treatment, how it has been formed or machined, whether there are welds, crevices, bolts, flanges or gaskets and so on. The environment is not just a matter of salt or fresh water. There are questions about the flow rate, whether there are suspended solids, whether the liquid is aerated or stagnant and so on.

This complexity is one reason why the subject requires a knowledge-based system integrated with a database rather than a stand-alone database system. The other consideration, which puts corrosion advice beyond the scope of a stand-alone database, is the fact that it is a process, not a property, and cannot be represented simply in terms of numbers.

Among the topics covered by the ACHILLES modules are:

- Marine corrosion.
- Paints and organic coatings.
- Metallic and inorganic coatings.
- Water treatment for heat exchanger systems.
- Corrosion monitoring and inspection.
- Atmospheric corrosion.
- Microbially-induced corrosion.
- Cathodic protection.

There are variations within and between modules, not only in the subject matter they cover but also in the way they interact with the user. In some cases it is appropriate for a module to give specific recommendations – for example, where the user is trying to select the most suitable material – but, in a dialogue about water treatment for a heat exchanger, it would be more appropriate for the system to indicate the various options which are available and, perhaps, introduce considerations which could affect the choice. If asked, "What are the design factors influencing corrosion in a heat exchanger?", the system would provide a list of design factors, acting in an informative rather than an advisory role.

ACHILLES has been created to run on IBM PCs, as this is the type of machine most widely available in design offices. When complete, ACHILLES will occupy about 10Mbytes of disk space and will have involved a total investment of the order of more than £400,000.

Some questions about giving the user the ability to make modifications – always a problem with expert systems – have not yet been resolved. The information provided by ACHILLES is generic, referring, for example, to types of paints rather than specific products. Individual companies may have a policy of buying certain paints from particular suppliers and may wish to incorporate their specifications in the system. Such a facility would have to be treated with very great care, both from Harwell's point of view and from the user company's point of view. For Harwell there would be the problem that an inexperienced user could corrupt the software and might be tempted to blame the supplier. For the user, if there is more than one copy of the software in use, there would be the problem of maintaining consistency between versions and avoiding unauthorised alterations.

PROTEUS – CLUB PROJECT ON LARGE-SCALE PROCUREMENT

CLUB projects, in which a number of companies collaborate in funding an expert system development, have a mixed reputation. Some of those supported by the government, under the Alvey programme, have been useful in giving their members better insight into the potential for expert systems but have not led to practical implementations. However, club projects can also be an attractive prospect for organisations which have an identifiable problem where an effective expert system would be valuable but where the risk of embarking on a new technology makes it difficult to justify the expense.

The first essential in establishing a successful club project is to bring together a number of organisations whose interests in developing an expert system are sufficiently close for them to agree on a common specification. The other essentials are to choose an experienced development organisation and to manage the project efficiently.

One post-Alvey club project, profiting from the experience of Alvey and which appears set to culminate in a successful system, is the

PROTEUS Club. This is a two-year project, sponsored by nine member organisations, which scheduled to have an operational expert system by March 1990. The system is intended to assist in major computer system procurement projects. A final prototype was tested and approved, on schedule, in February 1989 and development of the operational system proceeded satisfactorily, with user trials in late 1989 and early 1990.

The idea for an expert system to assist in large-scale procurement projects came from the STARTS Committee whose membership consists of government, public and commercial organisations that make use of large real-time computer systems. As a result, the Department of Trade and Industry (DTI) approached PA Consulting Group with a proposal for a club to which PA would be the contractor. The DTI was prepared to put up half the money, to a maximum of £200,000. Each member of the club would contribute £12,500 and the contractor would contribute, by means of subsidised fees, £70,000.

A preliminary meeting was held, in January 1986, to consider whether it was a proposal worth pursuing and PA prepared a discussion document which was presented at a public meeting, convened by the DTI, in October 1986. This produced a positive response, so a working party of the most enthusiastic organisations was set up and PA was commissioned to carry out a feasibility study. This study culminated in a prospectus, in April 1987, which was a reasoned open invitation to join the PROTEUS Club – the name is an acronym for 'procurement tender evaluation expert utility system'. After two more public meetings, and some strong persuasion, nine member organisations signed up and the project was started in February 1988.

Any initial reluctance to join the project was in no case related to the £12,500 membership fee – the main reason was that the project would occupy a lot of the participants' time. People were also uncertain about whether the end product would be really useful to them and this was understandable because the project was breaking new ground. The successful launch of the project owes a great deal to the enthusiasm of its steering group of member companies and the skill and determination of its chairman, Keith Holland, head of group purchasing at Midland Group. Other member organisations in the club are the Civil Aviation Authority, the Central Electricity Generating Board, IBM, the Ministry of Defence, the National Health Service, Peat Marwick McLintock Management Consultants and Royal Insurance (UK) – all organisations involved in very large purchasing projects.

ORGANISATION OF THE PROJECT

There are some potential pitfalls in a club project which need to be anticipated and avoided if it is to prove successful. One is that the differing needs of the members must be accommodated, as far as possible, and reconciled in a common purpose so that the project development team has a clear aim. Another potential pitfall is that clear distinctions must be maintained between the overall project management, the technical domain requirements of the end users – in this case procurement and computing specialists – and the technical aspects of the expert system design. In the case of the PROTEUS Club, the situation is further complicated by the interest of the DTI, as the provider of part of the finance, looking for a successful outcome in the public interest. These diverse concerns have been reconciled with the help of an organisation structure like that shown in Fig. 1.

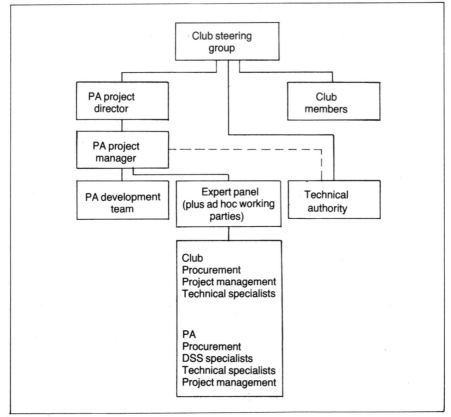

Fig. 1. PROTEUS Club organisation

At the hub of the organisation is the steering group, with senior representatives from all the member organisations, the DTI and PA. The chairman, vice chairman and secretary are all club members. This group, which meets for about two hours at three-monthly intervals, concerns itself, solely, with the progress of the project and allocation of resources and provides an interface between club members and the project managers. Bridging the gap between these meetings is the chairman's committee, consisting of the three steering group officers and the DTI and PA members.

Looking after the interests of the end users, by ensuring that the developed system will meet their requirements, is an expert panel consisting of about five people, all of them procurement specialists from the member companies. It is this panel which expresses a common user voice to the development team. It was responsible for approving the user requirements document, the functional specification and the prototype demonstrations. The expert panel meets when required but usually monthly.

Providing an authoritative evaluation of the specialist expert system design work of the development team is an independent technical authority, whose function is to provide a second opinion, to the steering group, on the technical quality of the work being done by the development team. This role is being very adequately fulfilled by a representative from the Royal Signals and Radar Establishment. This arrangement gives confidence to the club members that their interests are being looked after by an independent expert and avoids frustrating debates in committees.

PA's project team works under a project manager who is also highly experienced in procurement and is well able to appreciate the users' requirements.

DEVELOPMENT METHODOLOGY

The PROTEUS Club started with a budget of £365,000 and the project was planned in four stages:

- Preparing an outline specification.
- Prototyping the system and specifying the full system.
- Developing the operational system.
- User trials.

The outline 24-month timetable for the whole project is shown in

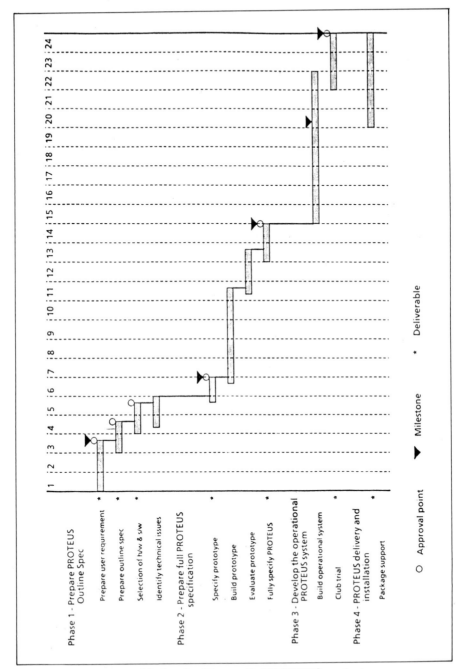

Fig. 2. Outline timetable for the 24-month PROTEUS project

Fig. 2. Production of the outline specification started with a statement of user requirements and culminated in a statement of the functions which the developed system would carry out and how it would operate. This was followed by decisions about the hardware and software to be used for the prototype and a specification for the prototype software.

The purpose of prototyping was not to produce a miniature version of the final operational system but to test any areas of uncertainty, where alternative approaches were possible, and to try out alternative ways of handling the user interfaces. It is quite difficult for a potential end user to visualise, in advance, what will be the most suitable interface for an application.

In the event there were three iterations of the prototyping process, each working from a formal specification and followed by a review. At the end of the second prototype development, the system was given a pilot trial – at Midland Bank, with users who had not been involved previously with the project.

Development of the prototypes was done on a TI Micro Explorer workstation, using the KEE Lisp environment which is very convenient for rapid development. The operational system is being developed using Common LISP on the IBM PS/2, which is more typically available in company procurement offices.

THE PROCUREMENT PROBLEM

The problems addressed by the system are those which occur in very large and technically or organisationally complex computer procurement projects, where procurement specialists, who are not computer experts, have to work alongside computer hardware and software experts who, in all probability, have never before been involved in a major procurement – and may never again be involved in one. Also the system is designed to support similar procurements in other application areas.

After a specification of user requirements has been drawn up, the company needs first to formulate a procurement strategy and to formulate a consistent method of stating the criteria by which any proposed system will be assessed. From these criteria, a large number of questions will be framed and incorporated in an 'invitation to tender' (ITT) document which will be sent to all potential suppliers. Also, before tenders are received from prospective suppliers, there will have to be decisions on the relative importance of the different questions and, hence, the weights to be attached to the answers.

In a major procurement project there will be very many aspects to be considered, leading, perhaps, to thousands of different questions in a hierarchical tree structure. The person managing the entire procurement project will need to check that every aspect has been considered thoroughly and the senior members of the procurement team will need to reach a consensus on the weightings to be applied to the different hardware and software elements in the proposed system.

When the tenders have been received from the prospective suppliers, they have to be evaluated against the previously determined criteria, giving each supplier 'scores' against each element of the project. These are accumulated to give scores right up to the top of the hierarchy. Next, the different suppliers must be compared with each other, their relative merits and demerits analysed and a conclusion reached as to the best tender. Finally, a statement has to be prepared indicating the strengths and weaknesses of the different tenders and the preferred supplier.

During this evaluation process, the procurement manager needs to be assured that all the members of the team are carrying out their evaluations consistently and to uniform standards and that any bias towards a particular supplier or feature is highlighted and investigated. Any hidden extra costs also need to be revealed and there must be ways of comparing different types of solutions offered by different suppliers. Fig. 3 illustrates the main steps in the tender evaluation process.

HOW THE SYSTEM WILL HELP

The system will function to help experts in their decision-making, rather than making decisions itself, and it will provide a framework within which the knowledge, relevant to a particular application, can be represented. Like other expert systems it comprises a knowledge base, built from the personal experiences of the people participating in the procurement project, an inference engine, supplying the reasoning mechanisms to be applied to this knowledge, and facilities for presenting and explaining the conclusions and advice offered by the system.

The system will give support throughout the tendering process but, particularly, in the setting and application of selection criteria. First, it will provide the opportunity for building a tree structure of criteria

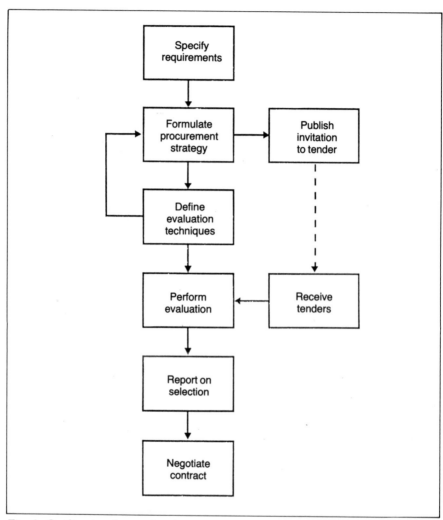

Fig. 3. Outline tender evaluation process

against which the proposed computer system will be measured. The highest levels of such a hierarchy might be something like that in Fig. 4. There may be 1,000 such criteria in a large project.

Another hierarchy is that of the evaluation teams which will be deciding on the criteria and their relative weights and which will be evaluating the responses from suppliers. PROTEUS envisages a high-level team, responsible for deciding on the broad areas of evaluation to be undertaken, and specialist teams, responsible for carrying out the evaluation process in each of the areas distinguished by the high-

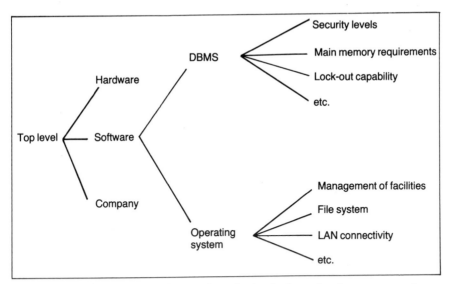

Fig. 4. Highest levels of a hierarchy of criteria for selecting a computer system

level team.

All of the criteria will have weightings attached to them. The weights, providing an indication of the relative importance to be given to different criteria at the same level of a sub-tree, are expressed in a simple numerical form (30%, 70%). Rules for combining the weightings at different levels of the hierarchy are held within the system which can show the consequences, at all levels, of a particular pattern of weights.

As the complex structure of criteria and associated questions develops, the procurement manager can see, from the display screen or print-outs, how the many aspects of the project are being covered by criteria, and their associated questions, and how the weights will affect the overall assessment. The high-level team can make adjustments in the light of this overview. The finally agreed set of criteria and questions can then be printed out as a file which can form part of the ITT document going out to prospective suppliers.

When the responses come in from prospective suppliers, the full evaluation teams will be set to work on them, each team dealing with a different group of criteria. The teams will match the responses from each supplier, separately, against the questions and will assign scores to each answer. Usually, more than one member of a team will make an independent assessment of the responses from each supplier so that, for every supplier, there will be two or more independent sets of scores, all of which go into the knowledge base.

From this information, the first type of analysis can be made, if required, checking for discrepancies between the scores of different evaluators and for differences in the relative assessments of different suppliers. This analysis can reveal a number of things. For example, it may show that a particular evaluator always tends to award above average scores – perhaps he does not like using the bottom end of the scale. One evaluator may regularly score a particular company higher than do other evaluators. This may indicate a bias or it may mean that the evaluator knows something the others do not. Analyses of this kind can be made by the system and presented to the procurement manager in tabular or graphical form. Analysis of this kind is not aimed at encouraging conformity to a norm in evaluation of responses but does mean that evaluators must be prepared to justify their opinions.

The next task for the system is to combine the different scores for each supplier into a set of consensus scores. The weightings are then applied to these scores to obtain weighted scores at each level up to the top of the hierarchy of criteria.

Some of the refinements to this process are worth mentioning here. Assigning a single number as a score for a supplier's response to a particular question may be unrealistic or undesirable, so there is also scope for giving a score in the form of a range, such as 60-80 (out of a possible 100). This approach can be taken further and scores can be given in linguistic form – 'average', 'very high' or 'good' – where range equivalents will previously have been assigned to the linguistic values. Where ranges are used, these are passed up the hierarchy so that the overall score for each prospective supplier will be presented in the form of a range.

For cases where a supplier has not answered a question, default scores can be assigned in advance or some other rule can be applied automatically. Scores greater than 100 may be acceptable where a supplier has exceeded requirements or a 'pass mark' may be assigned to a criterion where it is possible to decide whether a response is acceptable. Verbal comments can be added, by evaluators, to their scores and flagged to indicate the type of comment.

It often happens that individual suppliers can offer special features which may have a bearing on their overall rating, so the system has the ability to incorporate such features. In addition, sometimes a user may prefer not to specify requirements in too much detail, leaving scope for alternative technical solutions to be offered. The system has the flexibility to build in comparative assessments of different proposals.

In a project with many tenders it may be best to adopt a two-pass approach, using linguistic scoring to obtain a quick approximate evaluation of all potential suppliers, after which a short-listed group can be given a more detailed analysis.

At the end of this process, comparative evaluations are available for each prospective supplier – in detail at the bottom level of the hierarchy and in weighted, summarised form at the upper levels. The summarised results can be presented in tabular format or in the form of range histograms and a ranking of suppliers can be given on each of the main aspects of the proposed computer system.

WIDER SCOPE

The procurement system has been developed with particular types of procurement in mind – large hardware and software computer projects and similar types of procurement which are complex both technically and organisationally. However, there is nothing in it which restricts it to such applications – the tailoring to a particular procurement task is done by the user company in setting up the knowledge bases associated with the evaluation criteria, weightings and so on. PROTEUS Club members have ensured that PROTEUS will meet their computer procurement requirements but PA will also have the right to market the product independently and, it would appear, the system is applicable to any large procurement project involving several suppliers.

BENEFITS

There are a number of benefits which members of the PROTEUS Club expect to gain from using the system:

- *Consistency*. The system allows uniform procedures to be applied to supplier evaluations right across the project and for all prospective suppliers. In addition, it standardises the procedures for use in subsequent procurement projects.
- *Efficiency*. Procurement projects can be completed more quickly, with less effort and greater accuracy. Some users are already envisaging the introduction of multiple tendering in projects which are so large that this used to be considered impracticable.
- *Management control*. Probably for the first time, a procurement

manager will have the ability to see and control what is going on throughout a lengthy evaluation, even though teams may be scattered widely.

- *Detailed records.* In public sector procurement, particularly, there is a requirement to keep records of procurement decisions. In practice, record-keeping is often patchy and a crucial decision may be made with nothing put on record. The system automatically keeps a log of all the factors leading to decisions, and of the decisions themselves, in an easily accessible form in accordance with a draft European Community directive for Excluded Sectors.
- *Experience can be kept and re-used.* The criteria, questions and other value decisions from procurement projects can be modified and re-used in other similar projects, saving time and making the most of hard-won experience.
- *Training aid.* Trainee procurement specialists will be able to learn much from a re-run of earlier procurement projects.

All the above are direct benefits that can be expected from the introduction of a knowledge-based procurement evaluation system. In addition, there are further very large gains that can be expected as a result of the greater efficiency of tender evaluation:

- Better quality decisions will lead to the purchase of equipment, software and services that give better value for the money spent.
- Evaluation has been made with a particular benefit in view, such as reduced stock or faster introduction of new designs. As evaluation decisions are better informed, the final aim is more likely to be achieved and achieved more quickly.

Index